Guam

Travel Guide 2024

Your Essential Companion for Exploring the Natural Beauty, Outdoor Activities, History, and Culture

Lovelyn Hill

Dedication

I dedicate this guidebook to those captivated by the Guam. May it be your trusted companion through your remarkable visit to the West Pacific Ocean.

Table of Contents

Introduction

Welcome to the "Guam Travel Guide 2024: Your Essential Companion to Exploring the Natural Beauty, Outdoor Activities, History, and Culture." This meticulously crafted guide is designed to be your go-to resource for an enriching journey through Guam, providing a comprehensive overview of the island's captivating offerings. As you embark on this adventure, the guide aims to seamlessly integrate into your travel experience, offering insights and recommendations to make your exploration truly memorable.

In the heart of the Pacific, Guam beckons with a promise of diverse experiences that resonate with nature enthusiasts, adventure seekers, history buffs, and culture aficionados alike. The title of this guide encapsulates the essence of what awaits you – an essential companion that unfolds the myriad facets of Guam's charm.

Your journey begins with an invitation to delve into the allure of Guam's natural beauty. Pristine beaches, framed by azure waters, set the stage for relaxation and recreation. Discover the secrets of secluded coves and popular beachfront, where the symphony of waves provides a serene backdrop to your island sojourn. Engaging in water excursions offers not only a refreshing escape but also a chance to witness the vibrant marine life that thrives beneath the surface.

As you navigate Guam's landscape, lush forests, and wildlife beckon, inviting you to explore verdant wilderness. The guide sheds light on nature trails that wind through dense foliage, providing glimpses of unique flora and fauna. Wildlife encounters become an integral part of your journey, fostering a connection with the island's ecosystems and their delicate balance.

The scenic landscapes of Guam unfold like a living canvas, showcasing the island's diverse terrain. From panoramic views atop hills to picturesque valleys, each vista tells a story of Guam's geological beauty. For both avid photographers and those who simply appreciate breathtaking landscapes, these scenic wonders are sure to create lasting memories of your travels.

Moving beyond nature's wonders, Guam's rich history stands as a testament to its resilience and cultural heritage. Historical landmarks dot the island, narrating tales of colonial influences and pivotal moments. Cultural heritage sites invite you to delve into Guam's traditions, providing insights into the island's unique identity. Indigenous traditions are woven into the fabric of everyday life, and the guide illuminates the nuances of Chamorro culture, from vibrant festivals to time-honored customs.

Immersing in the local culture becomes a sensory journey through culinary delights, festivals, and traditional arts and crafts. Guam's gastronomic offerings reflect a blend of flavors, influenced by its multicultural history. Festivals and events pulse with the energy of celebration, inviting you to partake in the island's vibrant social sc. ne arts and crafts reveal the skilled hands and creative spirit of Guam's artisans, offering you a chance to take home a piece of the island's cultural legacy.

Practical travel information serves as the backbone of a seamless journey. Transportation tips, accommodation options, and essential travel essentials guide you in making informed decisions, ensuring that logistical details don't overshadow your exploration of Guam.

In the pages that follow, each section of this guide is tailored to enhance your experience, making it more than just a travel companion – it's your key to unlocking the best that Guam has to offer in 2024. So, as you flip through these pages, let the anticipation of discovery fuel your excitement, and may each chapter of Guam's story leave an indelible imprint on your travel narrative.

How to Use This Guide

Navigating through "Guam Travel Guide 2024" is a straightforward and enriching experience, ensuring that you make the most of your exploration of Guam. Here's a concise guide on how to effectively use this comprehensive travel companion:

Introduction to Sections

Begin by familiarizing yourself with the guide's sections, each dedicated to a specific aspect of Guam's allure, including natural beauty, outdoor activities, history, and culture.

Chapter Overviews

Dive into each chapter with a glance at the overviews provided. These summaries offer a snapshot of what to expect, allowing you to tailor your reading to your specific interests.

Focus on Your Interests

Given the diverse facets of Guam covered in this guide, focus on the sections that align with your interests. Whether it's pristine beaches, historical landmarks, or culinary delights, tailor your exploration to suit your preferences.

Practical Travel Information

The practical travel information section serves as a valuable resource for logistical details. Refer to transportation tips, accommodation options, and essential travel essentials to streamline your journey.

Interactive Recommendations

Throughout the guide, interactive recommendations are provided to enhance your experience. These may include suggested activities, must-visit locations, and insider tips to make your Guam adventure truly exceptional.

Enjoy the Journey

As you flip through the pages, immerse yourself in the rich content that unveils Guam's beauty. Let each recommendation guide you to memorable experiences, and don't hesitate to venture off the beaten path for your unique discoveries.

Remember, this guide is designed to be your companion, offering insights and recommendations that go beyond the surface. Embrace the adventure, explore with curiosity, and let the "Guam Travel Guide 2024" be your key to unlocking the vibrant essence of this Pacific gem.

Discover the Allure of Guam in 2024

In the heart of the Pacific Ocean, Guam beckons as a tropical haven ready to captivate your senses. Here's an extensive guide on why you should consider visiting Guam in 2024, delving into the diverse facets that make this island a compelling destination.

Diverse Natural Beauty

Guam's natural beauty is a symphony of vibrant hues and untouched landscapes that await your exploration. In 2024, you'll find yourself surrounded by pristine beaches with powdery white sands and crystal-clear waters. As you stroll along the shorelines, the gentle rhythm of the waves creates a soothing soundtrack to your island experience.

Venture into lush forests where emerald canopies embrace hidden trails. The air is thick with the fragrance of exotic flora, and the rich biodiversity of Guam's wildlife reveals itself as you navigate through these verdant wonders. Each step offers a chance to encounter the island's unique and captivating ecosystem.

The scenic landscapes of Guam paint a diverse canvas – from panoramic views atop rolling hills to the tranquil beauty of valleys. In 2024, you have the opportunity to witness these breathtaking vistas, creating moments that will forever be etched in your memory.

Thrilling Outdoor Adventures Await

For the adventure seeker, Guam in 2024 is an exhilarating playground. Dive into the world of adventure sports that add a touch of adrenaline to your island experience. Whether it's soaring through the sky on a zipline or conquering rugged terrains, Guam provides the perfect backdrop for your outdoor pursuits.

Water excursions beckon those eager to explore the marine wonders surrounding the island. Snorkeling in crystal-clear lagoons, diving into vibrant coral reefs, and embarking on guided boat tours promise an immersive aquatic adventure. Hiking trails wind through Guam's diverse landscapes, offering a chance to connect with nature on foot while discovering hidden gems along the way.

Rich Historical Narratives Unfold

Guam's history is a captivating blend of colonial influences and cultural resilience. In 2024, explore the island's historical landmarks that stand as silent witnesses to pivotal moments. From ancient Chamorro sites to relics from World War II, each landmark tells a story that contributes to Guam's rich historical narrative.

Cultural heritage sites invite you to step into the past, offering insights into Guam's unique identity. Museums and exhibits showcase artifacts that provide a glimpse into the island's multifaceted history. In 2024, these cultural gems invite you to delve deeper into the roots of Guam's heritage.

Immerse Yourself in Chamorro Culture

One of the highlights of visiting Guam in 2024 is the opportunity to immerse yourself in the indigenous Chamorro culture. The island comes alive with vibrant festivals and events celebrating its cultural richness. Engage in traditional dances, savor local delicacies, and participate in rituals that have been passed down through generations.

Beyond the festivities, Guam's local culture is woven into everyday life. The warmth of the people, their stories, and the creative expressions of traditional arts and crafts add depth to your experience. In 2024, you'll find yourself not just observing but actively participating in the vibrant culture of Chamorro.

Culinary Delights

Guam's culinary scene is a fusion of flavors influenced by its multicultural history. In 2024, embark on a gastronomic journey that tantalizes your taste buds with unique dishes. From local seafood delicacies to international cuisines, Guam's diverse culinary landscape offers a delightful experience for every palate.

Dynamic Festivals and Events Calendar

The year 2024 in Guam promises a dynamic calendar of festivals and events. Whether you're drawn to cultural celebrations, music festivals, or community gatherings, there's always something happening on the island. Dive into the lively atmosphere, connect with locals, and partake in the infectious energy that defines Guam's festive spirit.

Warm Hospitality and Local Interactions

Guam is renowned for its warm hospitality, and in 2024, you'll find the locals eager to share the best of their island. Engage in conversations, seek recommendations, and embrace the genuine friendliness that permeates every corner of Guam. The island's hospitality adds an extra layer of warmth to your journey, making you feel not just like a visitor but a welcomed guest.

2024 Travel Guide

As you plan your visit to Guam in 2024, the "Guam Travel Guide" serves as your personalized companion. Offering up-to-date insights and tailored recommendations, this guide ensures that you navigate the island seamlessly. From practical travel information to insider tips, let the guide be your key to unlocking the best that Guam has to offer.

Timeless Pacific Charm with a Modern Twist

Guam's allure lies in its timeless Pacific charm, yet 2024, it embraces modern influences. The blend of traditional and contemporary offerings creates a unique atmosphere, allowing you to experience the best of both worlds. Guam in 2024 is not just a destination; it's a dynamic and evolving island ready to be explored.

In conclusion, Guam in 2024 invites you on a journey that engages your senses, captures your adventurous spirit, and immerses you in a cultural experience that is both vibrant and authentic. So, pack your bags, embrace the warmth of the Pacific, and let Guam be the destination where your travel aspirations find fulfillment.

Chapter 1

Getting Acquainted with Guam

Island's Historical and Cultural Significance

Stepping onto the shores of Guam is akin to entering a living chronicle of the Pacific. This island, positioned in the western Pacific Ocean, carries a historical and cultural significance that spans centuries. As you explore Guam, you find yourself traversing through time, encountering remnants of a rich past that has shaped the identity of this Pacific gem.

Colonial Footprints

Guam's history bears witness to the influence of various colonial powers, and you, as a traveler, are set to explore the echoes of Spanish, American, and Japanese colonial periods. Historical landmarks such as Fort Nuestra Señora de la Soledad and the Plaza de España stand as tangible testaments to Guam's colonial legacy, offering glimpses into the struggles and triumphs that have defined the island.

World War II Impact

Guam played a pivotal role in World War II, and remnants of this tumultuous era are woven into its landscape. You find yourself standing amidst the haunting relics of war, such as the War in the Pacific National Historical Park, where remnants of bunkers and gun emplacements tell stories of resilience and sacrifice.

Chamorro Heritage

As you delve into Guam's cultural fabric, the Chamorro heritage emerges as a vibrant thread woven into everyday life. The indigenous Chamorro people contribute to the island's unique identity, preserving their traditions through dance, language, and art. Traditional villages like Inarajan and Talofofo offer immersive experiences, providing a glimpse into the daily lives of the Chamorro community.

Modern Developments and Attractions

Beyond its historical roots, Guam embraces modernity with a flair that captivates every visitor. The island's landscape is dotted with contemporary developments and attractions that seamlessly coexist with its cultural heritage.

Shopping Extravaganza

Guam is a shopping haven, offering a blend of international brands and local craftsmanship. Tumon, the island's commercial hub, beckons with duty-free shops, boutiques, and bustling markets. As you navigate through these retail havens, you're immersed in a shopping experience that mirrors Guam's diverse cultural influences.

Entertainment and Nightlife

When the sun sets, Guam transforms into a vibrant playground of entertainment and nightlife. From lively bars and clubs in Tumon to cultural performances at the Chamorro Village, you find an array of options to unwind and immerse yourself in the island's dynamic after-hours scene.

Modern Infrastructure

Guam's modern developments extend to its infrastructure, ensuring your stay is comfortable and convenient. You'll encounter well-maintained roads, efficient public transportation, and modern amenities in accommodation options ranging from luxury resorts to cozy guesthouses.

Family-Friendly Activities

If you're traveling with family, Guam offers a plethora of family-friendly activities. Water parks, wildlife encounters at the Cushing Zoo, and interactive museums like the Guam Museum cater to a diverse range of interests, making it an ideal destination for a memorable family vacation.

A Fusion of Past and Present

As you explore Guam's overview, it becomes evident that the island is a harmonious blend of its historical roots and contemporary developments. The juxtaposition of ancient traditions against a backdrop of modern infrastructure creates a unique ambiance that invites you to explore Guam not as a mere destination but as a captivating journey through time and progress.

Geographical Insights

Understanding Guam's Unique Geography

Guam, located in the western Pacific, is a captivating mosaic of landscapes that beckon exploration. As you embark on your journey, it's essential to grasp the unique geography that defines this island, shaping its character and offering a diverse range of experiences.

Island Dimensions and Location

Guam, measuring about 30 miles in length and 4 to 12 miles in width, is the largest and southernmost island in the Mariana Archipelago. Positioned approximately 3,800 miles west of Hawaii, Guam sits at the crossroads of Micronesia, Polynesia, and Melanesia, making it a hub of cultural diversity influenced by its strategic location.

Majestic Coastal Beauty

The island's coastline is a masterpiece of nature, featuring pristine beaches and rugged cliffs. From the white sands of Tumon Bay to the dramatic cliffs of Two Lovers Point, Guam's coastal beauty provides a stunning backdrop for relaxation and exploration.

Mesmerizing Coral Reefs

Guam's underwater world is equally enchanting, with coral reefs that teem with marine life. Snorkeling and diving enthusiasts are treated to a kaleidoscope of colors as they explore the vibrant coral gardens, home to a diverse array of fish and sea creatures.

Mariana Trench Proximity

Guam's unique geography is further accentuated by its proximity to the Mariana Trench, the deepest part of the world's oceans. While the trench itself is not visible from the surface, its influence on the island's geological features adds an intriguing dimension to Guam's allure.

Landmarks and Noteworthy Features

Beyond its natural splendors, Guam boasts landmarks and noteworthy features that serve as both cultural touchstones and navigational aids for travelers.

Mount Lamlam

As the highest point on the island, Mount Lamlam offers panoramic views that stretch across Guam's landscape. Whether you embark on a hike to the summit or appreciate the vistas from a distance, the allure of this natural landmark is undeniable.

Magellan's Landing Site

History comes to life at Umatac Bay, where explorer Ferdinand Magellan is believed to have made landfall in 1521. The landing site stands as a historical landmark, inviting you to connect with Guam's colonial past.

Latte Stone Park

Guam's indigenous Chamorro heritage is celebrated at Latte Stone Park, where ancient latte stones stand as silent witnesses to the island's pre-colonial history. These pillar-like stones, used as foundations for traditional Chamorro homes, are a testament to Guam's enduring cultural legacy.

Talofofo Falls

Nature takes center stage at Talofofo Falls, a cascading waterfall surrounded by lush greenery. Accessible through guided tours, the falls provide a tranquil escape and an opportunity to immerse yourself in Guam's natural beauty.

Asan Bay Overlook

For a poignant perspective on Guam's World War II history, the Asan Bay Overlook offers a solemn view of the Asan Invasion Beach. The overlook serves as a memorial to the sacrifices made during the war, providing a moment of reflection amidst the island's scenic grandeur.

As you absorb the geographical insights and landmarks of Guam, you'll find yourself on a journey that transcends mere exploration. Each corner of the island unfolds a narrative, inviting you to connect with the natural wonders and historical landmarks that make Guam a captivating destination in the heart of the Pacific.

Guam's Climate

Tropical Paradise All Year Round

Guam's climate is a defining feature, creating an idyllic tropical haven that beckons travelers seeking sun-drenched days and balmy evenings. As you plan your visit, understanding Guam's climate becomes pivotal, ensuring you make the most of the island's weather patterns.

Year-Round Tropical Warmth

Guam experiences a delightful tropical climate characterized by consistent warmth throughout the year. Regardless of when you choose to visit, you'll be greeted by temperatures that typically range from 75°F to 86°F (24°C to 30°C). This year-round warmth lays the foundation for a perpetual summer ambiance, inviting you to indulge in outdoor activities and coastal escapades regardless of the season.

Rainy Season and Typhoon Preparedness

Guam's climate is influenced by two distinct seasons: the dry season and the rainy season. The dry season, spanning from December to June, is characterized by lower humidity and minimal rainfall, providing optimal conditions for exploration and outdoor adventures. The rainy season, from July to November, introduces increased humidity and occasional heavy rainfall. During this period, Guam may also be susceptible to typhoons. It's essential to stay informed about weather forecasts and adhere to any safety advisories that may arise during this season.

Sea Breezes and Trade Winds

A delightful aspect of Guam's climate is the consistent presence of sea breezes and trade winds. These gentle winds create a refreshing atmosphere, particularly along the coastlines. Whether you're lounging on the beach or exploring outdoor attractions, the cool caress of these breezes adds a pleasant dimension to your Guam experience.

Best Time to Visit Guam

Guam, with its year-round tropical climate, offers a welcoming embrace to travelers at any time. However, understanding the nuances of the island's seasons can help you choose the ideal time for your visit, tailored to your preferences and the experiences you seek.

Dry Season (December to June)

December to February

The onset of the dry season brings a delightful reprieve from heavy rainfall, creating optimal conditions for outdoor activities and exploration. These months are considered the peak tourist season, attracting visitors seeking sunny days, warm temperatures, and clear skies. It's an ideal time for beach outings, water excursions, and immersing yourself in Guam's cultural and historical sites.

March to June

As the dry season progresses, March to June offers an extension of favorable weather conditions. During this period, Guam experiences pleasant temperatures, making it an excellent time for hiking trails, exploring natural landmarks, and indulging in the vibrant festivities that occasionally grace the island.

Shoulder Seasons (September to November and July to August)

September to November

Transitioning from the dry season to the rainy season, September to November marks Guam's shoulder season. While there might be occasional rainfall, the island remains lush and inviting. This period is characterized by a quieter atmosphere, providing an opportunity for a more serene and intimate exploration of Guam's attractions. It's an excellent time for nature enthusiasts who appreciate the verdant landscapes following occasional rain showers.

July to August

Midway through the rainy season, July to August maintains the island's warm temperatures while introducing intermittent rainfall. While this period may experience increased humidity, it offers a unique charm. The occasional rain showers contribute to the lush greenery, and it's an opportune time to enjoy the island's beauty in a more relaxed setting. If you're flexible and open to occasional rain, Guam in July and August provides a quieter ambiance.

Choosing Your Best Time

- For Sunny Days and Vibrant Atmosphere: The months of December to February are ideal, providing sunny days and a lively atmosphere. This period is well-suited for those seeking a classic tropical experience with optimal weather conditions.
- For a Quieter Experience: If you prefer a more tranquil environment and are open to occasional rainfall, the shoulder seasons of September to November and July to August offer a quieter Guam experience. You can still enjoy many of the island's attractions with fewer crowds.
- Considering Events and Festivals: Check Guam's event calendar, as various festivals and cultural events may influence your preferred travel dates. The island's vibrant festivities add an extra layer of excitement to your visit.

Ultimately, the best time to visit Guam depends on your personal preferences and the type of experience you desire.

Chapter 2

Natural Beauty

Pristine Beaches

Tumon Bay

Embark on your exploration of Guam's natural beauty by indulging in the idyllic shores of Tumon Bay. Located on the western shore of Guam, Tumon Bay stands out as a tropical oasis, offering a perfect blend of relaxation and vibrant activities.

Location

Tumon Bay is conveniently situated near the capital, Hagåtña, making it easily accessible for those staying in the central areas of Guam. You can reach Tumon Bay by a short drive from the major hotels and accommodations in the vicinity.

Beach Features

As you step onto the soft, white sand of Tumon Bay, you're greeted by crystal-clear turquoise waters that gently lap against the shore. The beach is fringed with lush greenery, providing a picturesque backdrop to your seaside retreat.

Amenities

Tumon Bay boasts a range of amenities catering to your comfort. Beachfront resorts and hotels offer easy access to the bay, with some providing beachside loungers and umbrellas for your leisure. You'll find nearby restaurants offering delectable local and international cuisines, allowing you to savor delightful meals with a view.

Activities

For water enthusiasts, Tumon Bay opens up a realm of aquatic adventures. Snorkeling and diving are popular activities, given the vibrant marine life thriving in the bay. Local operators provide equipment rentals and guided tours for an immersive underwater experience. Alternatively, take a stroll along the beach or engage in beach volleyball, embracing the dynamic energy of Tumon Bay.

Ritidian Point

For those seeking a more secluded beach escape, Ritidian Point beckons with its pristine shores and untouched beauty. Located on the northern tip of Guam, Ritidian Point offers a serene retreat surrounded by lush landscapes and rich biodiversity.

Location

Ritidian Point is situated in the northernmost part of the island, providing a tranquil haven away from the bustling tourist areas. While it may require a slightly longer drive, the journey is rewarded with the untouched beauty of this secluded beach.

Beach Features

As you set foot on Ritidian Point, the expansive stretch of white sand and the azure sea unfold before you. The beach is flanked by dense vegetation and offers panoramic views of the Pacific Ocean, creating a serene atmosphere.

Amenities

Given its natural and secluded setting, Ritidian Point has limited amenities. However, this is part of its charm, allowing you to immerse yourself fully in nature. Be sure to pack essentials such as water and snacks, as the beach area remains relatively undeveloped.

Activities

Ritidian Point serves as a sanctuary for those who appreciate nature and are passionate about wildlife. Take a leisurely walk along the shoreline, and you might encounter native wildlife, including sea turtles and diverse bird species. The beach also offers opportunities for picnics, allowing you to bask in the tranquility of this unspoiled coastal gem.

Ypao Beach Park

If you're traveling with family, Ypao Beach Park is an ideal destination, offering a family-friendly atmosphere with a range of amenities and activities for all ages.

Location

Conveniently situated in Tumon, Ypao Beach Park is easily accessible for families staying in the popular tourist areas. The proximity to shopping centers and dining options adds to the convenience of a day of beachside fun.

Beach Features

Ypao Beach boasts a wide sandy shoreline and shallow, calm waters, making it safe for families with children. The beach is equipped with grassy areas, providing spots for picnics and play.

Amenities

Ypao Beach Park is well-equipped with amenities to enhance your family day out. Restrooms, showers, and changing facilities are available, ensuring a comfortable experience. Beachside vendors offer snacks and refreshments, allowing you to stay fueled throughout the day.

Activities

Engage in a variety of water activities at Ypao Beach, from paddleboarding to kayaking. The serene waters create a perfect setting for beginners to experience water sports for the first time. The park also features playgrounds and open spaces, making it a perfect setting for family picnics and recreational games.

Yona Bay

Location

Discover the hidden gem of Yona Bay on the southeastern coast of Guam. This tranquil retreat provides an escape from the more bustling tourist areas, offering a serene atmosphere for those seeking quiet moments by the sea.

Beach Features

Yona Bay's charm lies in its simplicity and unspoiled beauty. The beach features golden sands and clear waters, providing an intimate setting for a peaceful getaway. Surrounded by lush greenery, Yona Bay creates a natural haven for relaxation.

Amenities

Given its more secluded nature, Yona Bay has limited commercial amenities. Consider packing a picnic and refreshments to fully enjoy the tranquility. The absence of crowds and commercial developments allows you to immerse yourself in the natural ambiance of the bay.

Activities

Yona Bay is perfect for those seeking a laid-back experience. Enjoy a leisurely swim in the calm waters or take a stroll along the shoreline. The beach's quietude makes it an ideal spot for contemplation and simply appreciating the beauty of the surroundings.

Agana Bay

Location

Situated near the capital city of Hagåtña, Agana Bay presents a harmonious blend of historical significance and natural beauty. Its strategic location offers easy access for those exploring the cultural heart of Guam.

Beach Feature

Agana Bay is unique for its blend of historical landmarks and coastal charm. The beach features a mix of sandy stretches and rocky outcrops, creating a picturesque scene. The panoramic views of the ocean and the skyline of Hagåtña add to the beauty of this bay.

Amenities

Agana Bay offers a range of amenities, including parks and scenic overlooks. The nearby capital city provides opportunities for exploration, with dining options and cultural sites within reach. The blend of natural beauty and historical elements makes Agana Bay a multifaceted destination.

Activities

Explore the historical aspects of Agana Bay by visiting nearby landmarks, such as Fort Soledad. Take a leisurely walk along the waterfront promenade, enjoying the views of the bay. The bay's accessibility to Hagåtña allows you to seamlessly integrate cultural exploration with beachside relaxation.

Tagachang Beach

Location

For those willing to venture off the beaten path, Tagachang Beach on Guam's western shore offers untouched tranquility. This hidden gem is nestled away from the more frequented areas, providing a serene escape.

Beach Features

Tagachang Beach captivates with its untouched beauty, featuring a mix of sandy stretches and rocky formations. The turquoise waters and coral-rich coastline make it a haven for snorkelers and nature enthusiasts. The beach's seclusion adds to its unspoiled charm.

Amenities

As a more secluded destination, Tagachang Beach has limited amenities. Plan accordingly by bringing essentials such as water and snacks. The absence of crowds allows you to relish the untouched beauty of the beach in a more intimate setting.

Activities

Immerse yourself in the natural wonders of Tagachang Beach by exploring the coral formations while snorkeling. Take a leisurely walk along the shore, appreciating the tranquility of this hidden coastal gem. Tagachang Beach offers a pristine escape for those seeking a more secluded and nature-centric beach experience in Guam in 2024.

As you consider your beach options in Guam, each destination offers a distinct experience, from historical charm to secluded tranquility. Whether you seek vibrant water activities, secluded natural beauty, or family-friendly fun, Guam's beaches are ready to be explored and enjoyed in 2024.

Chapter 3

Natural Beauty

Lush Forests and Wildlife

Guam's lush forests and diverse wildlife offer a haven for those seeking an immersive connection with nature. As you venture into these verdant landscapes, you'll discover a rich diversity of flora and fauna that defines Guam's unique ecological charm.

Inarajan Dos Amantes (Lovers' Point) Forest Reserve

Inarajan Dos Amantes Forest Reserve, a hidden gem on Guam's southern coast, beckons with its dense foliage and vibrant biodiversity. This reserve, known for its lush greenery and pristine environment, is an ideal starting point for your exploration of Guam's forests.

How to Get There

From central Guam, take the scenic route south on Route 4 towards Inarajan. Follow the signs leading to Dos Amantes and park in the designated area. The entrance is easily accessible, and the journey provides glimpses of Guam's rural charm.

Amenities

While the reserve is intentionally rustic, basic amenities like picnic areas and rest spots are available. Remember to bring your essentials, including water, snacks, and comfortable hiking gear.

Activities

Embark on nature trails that wind through the forest, offering serene walks and opportunities for birdwatching. Keep your eyes peeled for native species such as the Mariana Fruit Dove and Guam Kingfisher. The reserve also provides picnic spots, allowing you to savor the tranquility of the surroundings.

Tarzan Falls Trail and Wildlife Spotting

For a more adventurous exploration, the Tarzan Falls Trail in central Guam is a gateway to lush landscapes and cascading waterfalls. This trail not only immerses you in the island's greenery but also provides a chance to spot Guam's unique wildlife.

How to Get There

Located off Route 15, take the turn onto Cross Island Road (Route 17) and follow the signs for Tarzan Falls. Parking is available at the trailhead, and the hike begins through the heart of Guam's tropical forest.

Amenities

While the trail is relatively rugged, it offers a few designated rest areas. Carry essentials like water, insect repellent, and sturdy hiking shoes for a comfortable trek.

Activities

The trail leads you to the stunning Tarzan Falls, a picturesque waterfall surrounded by lush vegetation. Along the way, watch for the Micronesian Starling and other indigenous birds. The adventure includes wildlife spotting, adding an exciting element to your hike.

Facet of the Forest: Guam National Wildlife Refuge:

For a comprehensive wildlife encounter, Guam National Wildlife Refuge stands as a sanctuary for endangered species. Located in the northern part of the island, this refuge plays a crucial role in conservation efforts.

How to Get There

Access the refuge from Route 3, heading north. Clear signage directs you to the entrance. It's advisable to check the refuge's official website for any specific entry requirements or guided tour information.

Amenities

The refuge provides educational resources, and guided tours are available for a more in-depth experience. Ensure you carry essentials like water, a camera, and binoculars for bird watching.

Activities

Explore designated trails within the refuge to witness Guam's unique wildlife, including the Mariana fruit bat and the elusive Guam rail. Guided tours offer insights into conservation efforts and the significance of preserving Guam's ecological balance.

Tumon Bay Wildlife Sanctuary

Combining coastal beauty with wildlife encounters, Tumon Bay Wildlife Sanctuary is a testament to Guam's commitment to preserving its natural heritage. Located along the shores of Tumon

Bay, this sanctuary offers a different dimension to your exploration.

How to Get There

Accessible from the Tumon area, follow the coastal road towards Gun Beach. The sanctuary encompasses the coastal region, and signs indicate the protected areas.

Amenities

Tumon Bay offers amenities typical of a beach location, including nearby restaurants and facilities for water activities. It's an ideal spot for a relaxing day by the sea with added opportunities for bird watching.

Activities

Stroll along the bay, enjoying the coastal breeze and the view of the ocean. Birdwatchers can spot various seabirds, adding a touch of wildlife to the coastal scenery. For a more immersive experience, consider guided kayak tours that explore the sanctuary's marine and avian life.

Mount Santa Rosa Forest: A Hiker's Paradise:

For those seeking a more challenging hike amidst lush greenery, Mount Santa Rosa Forest provides an elevated perspective of Guam's natural beauty. This forested area, located in the central part of the island, offers panoramic views and diverse ecosystems.

How to Get There

Access Mount Santa Rosa from Route 17 (Cross Island Road). Follow the signs leading to the trailhead, and parking is available. The journey to the summit promises a rewarding exploration of Guam's elevated landscapes.

Amenities

While the trail itself may be rugged, the views from the summit make it worth the effort. Pack essentials such as water, snacks, and a camera to capture the breathtaking vistas.

Activities

Embark on the challenging yet fulfilling hike to the summit, where the dense forest gives way to commanding views of Guam's coastline. The trail offers opportunities for bird watching, with native species often spotted along the ascent. Photographers will find ample inspiration in the changing landscapes.

Pagat Cave and Surrounding Forest

Combining history with natural beauty, Pagat Cave and its surrounding forest in northern Guam offer a unique exploration. This area, with its limestone formations and lush vegetation, presents a captivating blend of geological wonders and ecological diversity.

How to Get There

Accessible from Route 15, follow the signs to Pagat Cave. Parking is available near the trailhead. The journey includes a hike through the forested area leading to the cave.

Amenities

The site is relatively rustic, so it's advisable to carry essentials for your hike, including water, sturdy footwear, and a flashlight if you plan to explore the cave.

Activities

Explore the trail leading to Pagat Cave, surrounded by dense vegetation and limestone formations. The cave itself holds historical significance, with ancient Chamorro artifacts discovered within. The surrounding forest provides an opportunity for quiet reflection amid nature's wonders.

Southern Mountains

Venture into Guam's southern mountains for a spectacular journey that includes the Cetti Bay Overlook. This region, characterized by dense forests and panoramic vistas, showcases the island's rugged beauty.

How to Get There

Accessible from Route 4, follow the signs to Cetti Bay Overlook. The drive takes you through picturesque landscapes before reaching the parking area.

Amenities

While the overlook offers breathtaking views, amenities are limited. Prepare for the journey with essentials such as water, comfortable clothing, and a camera.

Activities

Visit Cetti Bay Overlook for stunning views of southern Guam, surrounded by lush forests. The Southern Mountains also host hiking trails that provide deeper immersion into the island's tropical landscapes. Wildlife enthusiasts may spot indigenous birds and enjoy the serenity of this less-explored part of Guam.

Your exploration of Guam's lush forests and wildlife sanctuaries extends beyond the familiar trails, encompassing the challenging heights of Mount Santa Rosa, the historical significance of Pagat Cave, and the rugged beauty of the Southern Mountains. Each location not only reveals the ecological diversity of Guam but also offers a chance to connect with the island's heritage and untamed landscapes. As you traverse these natural wonders, let the richness of Guam's ecosystems unfold, creating a range of experiences that transcend the ordinary. Guam's lush forests and vibrant wildlife beckon you to discover the hidden corners of this Pacific paradise, where every step reveals a new facet of nature's wonders.

Scenic Landscapes

As you venture into the heart of Guam, the island's scenic landscapes unfold like mesmerizing paintings, each stroke revealing the diverse and captivating beauty of this Pacific gem.

Two Lovers Point (Puntan Dos Amantes)

Perched high above the Pacific Ocean, Two Lovers Point offers a breathtaking panoramic view. The cliffside location not only provides a stunning backdrop for photos but also immerses you in the romance of a Chamorro legend. Gaze across the vastness of the ocean as you feel the warm tropical breeze against your skin.

Cetti Bay Overlook

Nestled within the southern hills of Guam, the Cetti Bay Overlook presents a postcard-worthy panorama. The lush greenery surrounds the tranquil bay, creating a serene setting that invites you to appreciate the island's untouched beauty. It's an ideal spot to take in the natural symphony of waves and rustling leaves.

Mount Lam Lam

Ascending Mount Lam Lam, the highest peak on the island, rewards you with an awe-inspiring view. The panoramic vistas from this summit allow you to see Guam's diverse landscapes, from the sparkling coastline to the rolling hills. It's an excellent vantage point for capturing the island's grandeur.

Coastal Wonders

Tumon Bay

Tumon Bay, with its pristine white sandy beaches and crystal-clear waters, epitomizes the tropical paradise you've dreamed of. The bay's gentle curve is framed by lush greenery, creating a picturesque setting for strolls or a relaxing day by the water's edge.

Ritidian Point

For a more rugged coastal landscape, Ritidian Point beckons with its untamed beauty. The rocky shoreline, complemented by golden sand and turquoise waters, offers a raw and unfiltered connection to Guam's natural allure. You'll find a sense of solitude as you explore this untouched stretch of coastline.

Inland Marvels

Tarzan Falls:

A hidden gem within Guam's interior, Tarzan Falls is a testament to the island's diverse terrain. The falls cascade into a pristine pool, surrounded by lush vegetation. The journey to Tarzan Falls takes you through dense forests, unveiling Guam's rich biodiversity along the way.

Pagat Cave

Delve into the mystique of Pagat Cave, nestled along the northeastern coastline. This natural wonder combines coastal beauty with cave exploration. The entrance overlooks the Pacific, providing a unique blend of landscapes as you venture into the depths of the cave system.

Sunrise and Sunset Serenity

Cocos Island

If you're an early riser, Cocos Island offers an unparalleled sunrise experience. Located off the southern coast, this small island boasts coral reefs and white sandy beaches. As the sun ascends, casting hues of orange and pink across the sky, you'll witness a spectacle that marks the beginning of another day in paradise.

Asan Beach Park

As the day concludes, Asan Beach Park on Guam's western shore is a prime location to catch the sunset. The golden hour bathes the landscape in warm hues, creating a serene atmosphere. The historical significance of Asan Beach adds depth to the experience, providing a poignant moment of reflection as the sun dips below the horizon.

Guam's scenic landscapes, from cliffside viewpoints to coastal wonders and inland marvels, paint a vivid picture of the island's natural beauty. As you explore these panoramic vistas, each location becomes a chapter in your Guam adventure, revealing the diverse and captivating essence that defines this Pacific paradise.

Chapter 4

Outdoor Activities

Adventure Sports in Guam

Guam welcomes you to the heart-pounding realm of adventure sports where the island's natural beauty serves as the backdrop for an adrenaline-fueled journey. Whether you're a thrill-seeker or just looking to spice up your vacation, Guam in 2024 offers a spectrum of exhilarating activities that elevate your outdoor experience.

Soaring Heights with Skydiving

Dive headfirst into the excitement with skydiving adventures that offer unparalleled views of Guam's stunning landscapes. As you ascend to the skies, the island unfolds beneath you like a vibrant splendor. The rush of wind against your face and the expansive views create a sensory overload, making your descent an unforgettable moment suspended in time.

Dive into Aquatic Thrills

For those who prefer the embrace of the ocean, Guam's waters beckon with an array of aquatic adventures. Strap on your snorkel gear and explore the vibrant marine life thriving beneath the surface. Snorkeling in Guam is a kaleidoscopic experience, where coral gardens and diverse fish species paint an underwater masterpiece.

Surfing the Pacific Waves

Feel the power of the Pacific as you ride the waves along Guam's renowned surf spots. Whether you're a seasoned surfer or a beginner catching your first break, the island's beaches offer the perfect blend of challenge and thrill. Surf schools dotting the coastline provide expert guidance, ensuring you make the most of Guam's surf culture.

Scaling Heights in Rock Climbing

Venture into Guam's interior and discover the island's rugged terrain through rock climbing. With diverse climbing routes catering to all skill levels, you'll find yourself conquering peaks that offer breathtaking panoramic views. Guam's unique topography provides a natural playground for climbers seeking both challenge and reward.

Off-Road Adventures with ATV Riding

Embark on an off-road escapade as you navigate Guam's trails on an ATV. The island's diverse landscapes, from lush jungles to open fields, become the backdrop for your adrenaline-pumping ride. Rev up your engines and explore Guam's less-explored corners, where the thrill of off-road exploration meets the island's natural splendor.

Ziplining Across Scenic Vistas

For a bird's-eye perspective of Guam's beauty, engage in ziplining adventures that traverse lush canopies and scenic landscapes. As you soar through the air, the island unfolds beneath you, providing a unique and exhilarating perspective. Ziplining in Guam isn't just a thrilling activity; it's a visual feast for the senses.

Snorkeling with Sharks

Take a plunge into the Pacific waters for an extraordinary encounter with Guam's underwater residents. Snorkeling with sharks is a guided adventure that offers a safe and immersive experience with these magnificent creatures. The crystal-clear waters become a window to Guam's marine world, where sharks gracefully navigate their oceanic domain.

Aerial Views through Parasailing

Elevate your Guam experience with parasailing, where you'll soar high above the ocean while tethered to a parachute. The sensation of weightlessness combined with sweeping views of Guam's coastline creates a moment of serenity amidst the thrill. Parasailing is an ideal way to witness the island's beauty from a unique vantage point.

Caving Expeditions for the Bold

Delve into Guam's underground wonders with caving expeditions that unveil the island's geological marvels. As you navigate through limestone caverns adorned with unique formations, you'll be transported to a subterranean world filled with mystery. Caving in Guam is an adventure that merges exploration with the island's geological history.

In the realm of adventure sports, Guam isn't just a destination; it's a dynamic playground where nature and adrenaline converge. From soaring heights to exploring underwater realms, the island's offerings cater to every adventurer's desires. As you delve into

Guam's outdoor activities, let the thrill of each experience become a vibrant chapter in your journey through this Pacific paradise.

Water Excursions in Guam

As you explore the outdoor wonders of Guam, the chapter on water excursions opens the door to a world of maritime experiences that define the island's coastal charm. In 2024, Guam's azure waters become your playground, offering a range of aquatic activities that promise both relaxation and exhilaration.

Exploring Marine Marvels through Snorkeling

Dip beneath the surface and enter a realm of vibrant colors and marine wonders with Guam's snorkeling excursions. Explore coral reefs teeming with diverse fish species, as the warm Pacific waters envelop you in an underwater spectacle. Guided snorkeling tours ensure you uncover the best-kept secrets of Guam's coastal treasures.

Diving Adventures in the Pacific Depths

For a deeper immersion into Guam's marine world, scuba diving unveils a captivating realm beneath the waves. Explore underwater caves, and coral gardens, and encounter marine life in their natural habitat. The island's crystal-clear waters provide optimal visibility, creating an unforgettable diving experience for both novice and experienced divers.

Guided Boat Tours for Coastal Discovery

Embark on a guided boat tour to discover Guam's coastal beauty from a different perspective. Cruising along the island's shores, you'll witness dramatic cliffs, hidden coves, and pristine beaches.

Knowledgeable guides share insights into Guam's geography, marine life, and the cultural significance of coastal landmarks.

Kayaking Adventures Through Mangroves

Paddle through the serene waters of Guam's mangrove forests with a kayaking expedition. As you navigate through winding waterways, the lush mangroves create a picturesque backdrop. Kayaking offers a tranquil yet immersive experience, allowing you to connect with Guam's coastal ecosystems at your own pace.

Sunset Cruises for Romantic Seascapes

Indulge in the romance of Guam's sunsets with a leisurely sunset cruise. Glide across the Pacific waters as the sun dips below the horizon, casting a warm glow over the island. Sunset cruises provide an idyllic setting for couples or those seeking a serene and picturesque way to end the day.

Fishing Adventures in the Pacific Blue

For the angler at heart, Guam's deep-sea fishing charters offer an opportunity to cast your line into the Pacific blue. Whether you're a seasoned fisherman or trying your hand at fishing for the first time, the open waters around Guam are home to a variety of game fish, promising an exciting and rewarding day at sea.

Jet Skiing for High-Speed Thrills

Feel the rush of the ocean breeze as you zoom across Guam's waters on a jet ski. Jet skiing provides a burst of adrenaline, allowing you to explore the coastline with speed and agility. Rent a jet ski and carve your path along Guam's shores, creating your aquatic adventure on the fly.

Snuba Diving for an Underwater Experience

For those seeking a middle ground between snorkeling and scuba diving, Guam offers snuba diving. Dive with ease using a breathing apparatus connected to a floating raft, allowing you to explore underwater wonders without the need for heavy dive gear. Snuba diving is an accessible way to experience Guam's marine biodiversity.

Submarine Tours for Oceanic Exploration

Delve into the depths of the Pacific without getting wet through submarine tours. Board a submersible vessel and descend into Guam's underwater world, where large windows provide unobstructed views of marine life and coral formations. Submarine tours offer a unique and comfortable way to explore the ocean's mysteries.

Hiking Trails in Guam

Step into the lush heart of Guam as you explore the island's diverse landscapes through its captivating hiking trails. In 2024, Guam invites you to lace up your hiking boots and venture into terrains that reveal the island's rich biodiversity, panoramic vistas, and the essence of its unspoiled beauty.

Ancient Trails of Two Lovers Point

Embark on a cultural journey as you tread the trails leading to Two Lovers Point. Wrapped in legend and history, this hike not only offers spectacular views of the coastline but also connects you with Guam's folklore. As you ascend, the whispers of the past accompany you, creating an immersive journey through time.

Talofofo Falls

Immerse yourself in the lush greenery surrounding Talofofo Falls. The hiking trail to the falls winds through a pristine rainforest, revealing the untamed beauty of Guam. The cascading waters of Talofofo Falls become a rewarding spectacle at the end of your trek, providing a tranquil retreat amidst nature's splendor.

Fonte Plateau

Traverse the Fonte Plateau hiking trail, where history and nature intertwine seamlessly. This route takes you through ancient Chamorro latte stone pillars, remnants of Guam's indigenous past. The panoramic views from the plateau offer a glimpse into the island's topography, making it a hike that encapsulates both cultural and natural heritage.

Mount Lamlam

Challenge yourself with a hike to the summit of Mount Lamlam, the highest point in Guam. The trail unfolds through varying landscapes, from dense forests to open ridges, offering a diverse hiking experience. Reach the summit and be rewarded with breathtaking views encompassing the island and beyond, marking your achievement at Guam's pinnacle.

Lost Pond

Embark on a trail leading to the secluded oasis of Lost Pond. Tucked away amidst Guam's foliage, this hidden gem provides a serene escape. The hike itself becomes a journey of discovery, as the trail meanders through flourishing vegetation, creating an intimate connection with Guam's unexplored corners.

Facpi Ridge

Discover the beauty of Guam's coastal panoramas along the Facpi Ridge trail. As you hike, the trail offers glimpses of the Pacific Ocean and the island's dramatic cliffs. This trek is a visual feast, showcasing the intersection of land and sea, making it a must for those seeking a scenic and invigorating hiking experience.

Pagat Cave

Embark on a spelunking adventure as you hike to Pagat Cave, nestled along Guam's northeastern coastline. The trail takes you through limestone formations and dense foliage, eventually revealing the entrance to the cave. Inside, the cavernous space unfolds, creating a sense of wonder as you explore this unique subterranean world.

Ga'an Point

Meander along the coastal trails of Ga'an Point, where the rhythmic sounds of the Pacific accompany your hike. This trail offers a balance between coastal tranquility and captivating landscapes. The gentle sea breeze and the rustle of palm fronds become your companions as you explore Guam's scenic coastal paths.

Making Each Step Count

As you embark on Guam's hiking trails, each step becomes a brushstroke on the canvas of your island adventure. Whether you're drawn to the cultural significance of ancient trails or the challenge of summiting Guam's highest peak, the hiking trails in 2024 invite you to be both an explorer and a part of the island's natural narrative. Let the trails guide you through an immersive journey, uncovering the beauty and diversity that define Guam's terrestrial landscape.

Chapter 5

Exploring Guam's Rich History

Historical Landmarks

Guam, steeped in history and rich cultural heritage, boasts an array of historical landmarks that narrate compelling stories of the island's evolution. As you embark on this historical exploration, each landmark unveils layers of Guam's past, providing a tangible connection to the events and influences that have shaped the island.

Latte Stone Park

Latte Stone Park stands as a symbolic guardian of Chamorro heritage, showcasing the ancient pillars that once supported traditional Chamorro houses. Located in Hagåtña, the park invites you to witness the sheer magnitude of these ancient stones, offering insight into the architectural prowess of Guam's indigenous people. As you stroll through the park, the Latte Stones stand proudly, echoing tales of the Chamorro way of life and the resilience of a community deeply rooted in its traditions.

Fort Nuestra Señora de la Soledåd

Venture to Umatac and discover Fort Nuestra Señora de la Soledåd, a fortress that stands testament to Guam's Spanish colonial era. Originally constructed in the late 17th century, this historical gem provides a glimpse into Guam's strategic significance during Spanish rule. As you explore the remnants of this fortress, you are transported back in time, envisioning a period when Fort Soledåd served as a vital stronghold overlooking Umatac Bay.

Plaza de España

Stroll through the heart of Hagåtña and find yourself in Plaza de España, a colonial square that echoes with the footsteps of centuries past. Flanked by historical buildings, this plaza was once the administrative center of Guam during the Spanish era. Today, it serves as a tranquil space for reflection, surrounded by the Governor's Palace, the Dulce Nombre de Maria Cathedral-Basilica, and the historic Almacen (Storehouse). Plaza de España encapsulates the colonial charm that continues to resonate through modern Guam.

Altepetl de Agana

Delve into the cultural essence of Guam at Altepetl de Agana, a sacred site that holds deep significance for the Chamorro people. This ancient village site, located in Hagåtña, represents the historic and spiritual core of the Chamorro civilization. As you explore the remains of ancient latte stones and village structures, you connect with the enduring spirit of the Chamorro ancestors, gaining a profound understanding of Guam's indigenous roots.

Jeff's Pirates Cove

While Guam's history is marked by periods of colonization, it also bears the indelible imprints of World War II. Jeff's Pirates Cove, situated in Talofofo, serves as a living testament to this tumultuous era. Originally a Japanese radio station during the war, the site

44

transformed into a popular beachside haven. Today, as you enjoy the panoramic views of Apra Harbor, you can almost hear the echoes of history, envisioning the strategic significance this area held during wartime.

Inarajan Pools

Journey to the southeastern coast of Guam and discover the mystical Inarajan Pools, a site steeped in ancient Chamorro traditions. Used for various ceremonies and rituals, these natural rock pools are surrounded by lush greenery and offer breathtaking views of the Pacific Ocean. As you stand by these pools, you can almost feel the spiritual energy of the Chamorro people, connecting with a heritage that has withstood the test of time.

Sumay Cemetery

Sumay Cemetery stands as a somber reminder of the forced evacuation of the village of Sumay during World War II. Located near Naval Base Guam, this cemetery holds the remains of the original Sumay residents. As you wander through this poignant site, you can sense the weight of history, reflecting on the resilience of the Chamorro people in the face of wartime challenges.

Ritidian Point

Explore Ritidian Point, located at the northern tip of Guam, and witness the remnants of ancient Chamorro village life. This archaeological site features latte stones, pottery shards, and other artifacts, providing a glimpse into the daily lives of Guam's indigenous people. As you stand amidst the ancient foundations, the whispers of Chamorro ancestors resonate, offering insight into the island's pre-colonial heritage.

Spanish Bridge in Umatac

Step onto the Spanish Bridge in Umatac, an architectural marvel that spans the Talofofo River. Constructed during Spanish rule, this bridge serves as a symbolic connection between Guam's past and present. As you traverse its weathered stones, consider the significance of this structure in facilitating communication and trade during the colonial era.

Asan Bay Overlook

Visit Asan Bay Overlook, a site that commemorates the Liberation of Guam during World War II. Offering panoramic views of Asan Beach and the Pacific Ocean, this overlook stands as a tribute to the sacrifices made by the Allied forces and the enduring spirit of the Chamorro people. As you gaze upon the serene waters, reflect on Guam's journey from occupation to liberation and the resilience that defines its history.

Magellan Monument

Discover the Magellan Monument in Umatac, a tribute to the renowned explorer Ferdinand Magellan. Erected to commemorate his visit to Guam in 1521, this monument symbolizes the early interactions between European explorers and the Chamorro people. As you stand by this historical marker, consider the pivotal role Guam played in the age of exploration and the subsequent waves of cultural exchange.

Chief Gadao's Cave

Uncover Chief Gadao's Cave in Inarajan, a geological marvel intertwined with Chamorro folklore. Legend has it that Chief Gadao, a revered Chamorro leader, sought refuge in this cave during times of conflict. Explore the cave's natural formations and

46

feel the echoes of ancient tales resonating through the chambers, offering a glimpse into the cultural narratives that shape Chamorro's identity.

Hagåtña River Walk

Embark on a stroll along the Hagåtña River Walk, immersing yourself in the heart of Guam's capital. Lined with historical markers and monuments, this scenic walkway encapsulates the island's colonial history and cultural vibrancy. As you meander along the riverbanks, absorb the ambiance of Hagåtña, where each step unveils a new facet of Guam's diverse heritage.

Two Lovers Point

Visit Two Lovers Point, an iconic landmark that transcends history and folklore. Perched on a cliff overlooking Tumon Bay, this site is tied to a tragic legend of two lovers who chose to leap from the cliffs rather than face separation. The monument celebrates eternal love and serves as a poignant reminder of Guam's cultural stories, inviting you to witness the breathtaking views and reflect on the enduring power of love.

Cultural Heritage Sites

Guam's cultural heritage sites offer a captivating journey into the island's identity, reflecting the rich traditions, rituals, and artistic expressions that define Chamorro culture. As you explore these sites, you'll gain profound insights into Guam's unique cultural heritage.

Inarajan Village

Nestled on Guam's southeastern coast, Inarajan Village stands as a living museum of Chamorro traditions. The village, with its traditional thatched-roof huts known as "guma' chånan lina'la'," invites you to step back in time. Wander through the village lanes adorned with colorful flora, where the air is infused with the scents of incense and the echoes of ancient Chamorro chants linger. Inarajan Village provides an immersive experience, allowing you to witness and participate in traditional dances, weaving, and other cultural practices that have endured through generations.

Dulce Nombre de Maria Cathedral-Basilica

Located in Hagåtña, the Dulce Nombre de Maria Cathedral-Basilica is not only a place of worship but also an architectural masterpiece that bears witness to Guam's enduring Catholic heritage. As you stand before its towering façade, adorned with intricate carvings and stained glass, you'll sense the spiritual significance that has been woven into the very fabric of Guam's history. The cathedral's interiors, with their solemn ambiance, showcase religious art and artifacts that narrate the story of faith on the island.

Guam Museum

Perched atop Skinner Plaza in Hagåtña, the Guam Museum serves as a cultural beacon, offering a comprehensive narrative of Guam's history. This modern institution features exhibitions that span pre-colonial Chamorro culture to the island's colonial periods and beyond. Explore the galleries that house artifacts, artworks, and interactive displays, each providing a deeper understanding of Guam's cultural evolution. The museum serves as a bridge between the past and the present, fostering a sense of pride and connection for both residents and visitors.

Sågan Kotturan Chamoru

Venture to Tumon and discover Sågan Kotturan Chamoru, a center dedicated to preserving and promoting Chamorro arts and crafts. This cultural hub showcases traditional and contemporary Chamorro artworks, including carvings, paintings, and pottery. As you explore the exhibits, you'll witness the diverse expressions of Chamorro's creativity, providing a visual journey through the island's artistic heritage. Sågan Kotturan Chamoru serves as a testament to the vibrancy of Guam's cultural identity.

Chief Quipuha Park

Chief Quipuha Park, situated in Agat, pays homage to Chief Quipuha, a respected Chamorro leader during the Spanish colonial era. The park features a monument and interpretive displays that highlight Chief Quipuha's significance in Chamorro history. The serene surroundings offer a contemplative space to reflect on the leadership and resilience embedded in Guam's cultural heritage.

Gef Pa'go Chamorro Cultural Village

Embark on a cultural odyssey at Gef Pa'go Chamorro Cultural Village in Inarajan. This living museum showcases traditional Chamorro homes, ancient latte stones, and artifacts, providing an immersive experience of Chamorro life. Participate in cultural demonstrations, from coconut husking to traditional cooking, and gain firsthand knowledge of the practices that have sustained Chamorro culture for centuries.

Sanctuary Inc. Folk Art Gallery

Head to the village of Dededo and explore the Sanctuary Inc. Folk Art Gallery, a haven for Chamorro craftsmanship. The gallery features intricately crafted artifacts, including woven baskets, pottery, and jewelry. Each piece tells a story of skill, tradition, and cultural pride. The Sanctuary Inc. Folk Art Gallery is not just a showcase; it's a celebration of the artisans who contribute to the preservation of Chamorro's cultural heritage.

Indigenous Traditions

Guam's indigenous traditions are woven into the very fabric of the island, reflecting the Chamorro people's deep connection to their ancestral roots. As you explore Guam's indigenous traditions, you'll uncover a cultural richness woven with rituals, customs, and a profound sense of identity.

Taotaomo'na

The belief in Taotaomo'na, spirits of ancestors, is a cornerstone of Chamorro spirituality. These ancestral spirits are believed to reside in ancient trees, caves, and other sacred places. As you explore the island, pay homage to these spirits by approaching such sites with respect. The ancient trees, known as "ifil," hold stories whispered through the wind, and the caves, like those in Pagat, resonate with the echoes of Chamorro spirituality.

Chamorro Seafaring

The art of Chamorro seafaring is an enduring tradition that harks back to ancient navigators who skillfully sailed the Pacific using celestial cues and knowledge passed down through generations. While you may not be navigating the open seas yourself, a visit to the Chamorro Seafaring Heritage Center in Umatac offers a glimpse into this rich maritime legacy. Explore the exhibits, which showcase traditional canoes, navigation tools, and the remarkable skills that allowed Chamorro ancestors to traverse vast ocean expanses.

Hålomtåno'

Hålomtåno', or traditional Chamorro healing, is deeply rooted in the use of natural remedies and spiritual practices. Engage with this ancient healing tradition by visiting local healers or participating in wellness events that showcase Chamorro herbal remedies. The forests of Guam are abundant with medicinal plants, and the knowledge of hålomtåno' practitioners carries the essence of centuries-old healing practices.

Gupot Chamorro

Gupot Chamorro, or Chamorro celebrations, mark significant life milestones such as births, weddings, and graduations. Experience the vibrant festivities by attending local events or celebrations during your visit. These joyous occasions often feature traditional dances, feasts, and the sharing of local delicacies, providing a firsthand encounter with the warmth and communal spirit inherent in Chamorro celebrations.

Chamorro Language

The Chamorro language serves as a linguistic vessel that carries the cultural identity of Guam. While English is widely spoken, the preservation of the Chamorro language remains crucial. Immerse yourself in the linguistic heritage by attending language workshops or engaging in conversations with locals who cherish and speak Chamorro fluently. The nuances of the language reveal insights into Chamorro's thoughts, expression, and the unique way in which the island's indigenous people communicate.

Tasa

Journey to the village of Agat and encounter the Tasa, a traditional Chamorro canoe house. This cultural center is a hub for preserving and sharing indigenous knowledge, including traditional navigation, arts, and crafts. Engage with local experts who passionately share insights into Chamorro traditions, offering a firsthand experience of the wisdom passed down through generations.

Ancestral Lands

The concept of Taotao Tåno', the people of the land, is deeply ingrained in Chamorro culture. Respect for ancestral lands is a vital aspect of indigenous traditions. As you explore the island, be mindful of designated cultural sites and natural areas. These sacred places, such as Fouha Rock and Pagat Cave, hold spiritual significance and are integral to preserving the Chamorro way of life.

Chapter 6

Immersing in the Local Culture

Culinary Delights

Guam's culinary scene is a sensory journey that invites you to savor a delightful fusion of flavors influenced by its multicultural history. From local street vendors to renowned restaurants, Guam's culinary delights promise a gastronomic adventure that captivates your taste buds.

Chamorro BBQ at Chamorro Village

Dive into the heart of Chamorro culture with a visit to Chamorro Village, a bustling market where the air is filled with the enticing aroma of grilled delicacies. The Chamorro BBQ stalls offer an array of tantalizing meats, marinated to perfection and cooked on open grills. Savor skewers of succulent chicken, pork, and beef, each infused with a unique blend of local spices. Prices typically range from $3 to $10, providing an affordable and delectable dining experience.

Red Rice and Kelaguen at Meskla Dos

Meskla Dos, a popular local eatery, beckons you to savor two Chamorro staples – red rice and kelaguen. Red rice, a vibrant side dish, is a flavorful blend of rice, annatto seeds, and various seasonings. Complementing this, kelaguen is a traditional Chamorro dish featuring diced meat, often chicken or fish, marinated in lemon juice, coconut, and hot peppers. The combination of the two at Meskla Dos provides a taste of Guam's authentic culinary heritage, with prices ranging from $8 to $15.

Seafood Extravaganza at Proa Restaurant

For an exquisite seafood experience, Proa Restaurant stands out as a premier dining destination. Overlooking Tumon Bay, Proa offers a seafood extravaganza featuring the catch of the day. Indulge in lobster, shrimp, and a variety of fish prepared to perfection. The menu's seafood options range from $20 to $50, offering a premium dining experience with a view that complements the delectable flavors.

Boonie Pepper Water at Jeff's Pirates Cove

Jeff's Pirates Cove, nestled along the coastline, invites you to try the local favorite – Boonie Pepper Water. This Chamorro soup, infused with spicy boonie peppers, coconut milk, and various herbs, provides a unique and bold flavor. Pair it with fresh seafood or local meats for an authentic Guam dining experience. A bowl of Boonie Pepper Water at Jeff's Pirates Cove typically costs between $10 and $15.

Latte Stone Ice Cream at The Guam Food Guy's Cafe

Complete your culinary journey with a sweet treat – Latte Stone Ice Cream. The Guam Food Guy's Cafe introduces you to this delightful dessert inspired by Guam's iconic latte stones. Indulge in flavors like coconut, mango, and ube, all crafted with local ingredients. A scoop of Latte Stone Ice Cream is a refreshing way to conclude your gastronomic exploration, priced between $3 and $5.

Sizzling Fai Doa at Pika's Café

Pika's Café introduces you to the sizzling delight of Fai Doa, a dish that exemplifies the fusion of Chamorro and Filipino influences. Fai Doa consists of marinated pork belly or chicken, grilled to perfection and served with a side of garlic fried rice. The savory aroma and bold flavors make it a must-try dish, and prices typically range from $12 to $18.

Tumon Bay Tacos at The Beach Bar & Grill

Indulge in Tumon Bay Tacos at The Beach Bar & Grill, a beachfront gem offering a picturesque setting for your culinary adventure. These tacos feature local fish or shrimp, seasoned with Guam's unique flavors and served with a medley of fresh vegetables. Enjoy this delightful beachside dining experience with prices ranging from $10 to $20.

Chicken Kelaguen Pizza at Delmonico Kitchen + Bar

Delight your taste buds with a unique twist on traditional Chamorro flavors at Delmonico Kitchen + Bar. The Chicken Kelaguen Pizza combines the zest of kelaguen with the comfort of pizza, featuring grilled chicken, lemon, coconut, and hot peppers atop a crisp crust. This culinary fusion is a testament to Guam's creativity, with prices ranging from $15 to $25.

Tinala Katne at The Enclave

The Enclave introduces you to Tinala Katne, a dish that pays homage to Guam's preserved meat tradition. Tinala Katne involves curing and smoking thin slices of beef, resulting in a flavorful and savory treat. Served with red rice and finadene sauce, this dish offers a unique taste of Guam's culinary heritage, with prices typically ranging from $15 to $25.

Chamorro High Tea at LÅGU Coffee & Chamorro Cuisine

Elevate your Guam dining experience with Chamorro High Tea at LÅGU Coffee & Chamorro Cuisine. This unique experience combines the elegance of high tea with Chamorro flavors, featuring local teas, savory bites, and Chamorro-inspired pastries. Immerse yourself in this culinary adventure, with prices for Chamorro High Tea starting from $25.

Gåyi at Street Market Food Stalls

For a quick and flavorful street food experience, seek out Gåyi at local market stalls. Gåyi is a popular Chamorro dish featuring chicken or beef skewers marinated in a savory soy sauce and grilled to perfection. These affordable delights, priced between $5 and $10, offer a convenient and tasty option as you explore local markets.

Gef Pa'gon at Meskla on the Cove

Meskla on the Cove introduces you to Gef Pa'gon, a Chamorro dish that showcases the island's seafood bounty. This coconut-based soup features shrimp, crab, and a medley of vegetables, creating a rich and flavorful culinary experience. Dive into the island's seafood heritage with prices ranging from $15 to $30.

Local Craft Beer at The Guam Brewery

Complement your Guam culinary journey with locally brewed craft beer at The Guam Brewery. The brewery offers a range of unique flavors, inspired by Guam's tropical surroundings. Enjoy a refreshing pint while soaking in the laid-back atmosphere, with prices for local craft beer starting from $6.

Night Market Delicacies

Experience the vibrant energy of the Guam Night Market, where local vendors showcase an array of culinary delights. From coconut desserts to savory empanadas, the night market offers a diverse selection of street food. Prices vary, providing an affordable option for those looking to sample a bit of everything in this lively culinary setting.

Fresh Produce at Chamorro Farmers' Market

Immerse yourself further in Guam's culinary scene by exploring the Chamorro Farmers' Market. Here, you'll find an abundance of fresh produce, including tropical fruits, herbs, and spices. Engage with local farmers and vendors to discover the essence of Guam's agricultural landscape while purchasing ingredients to recreate Chamorro dishes in your style.

In closing, Guam's culinary landscape unfolds as a gastronomic adventure, with each dish telling a story of cultural fusion and creativity. As you explore the island's diverse dining establishments, let your taste buds be your guide, and enjoy the flavors that make Guam's culinary scene a rich and evolving range of taste.

Festivals and Events

Guam's calendar is brimming with lively festivals and events that add a vibrant rhythm to the island's cultural scene. As you plan your visit in 2024, consider aligning your itinerary with these engaging celebrations:

Liberation Day Festival (July 21-22)

Join the island-wide celebration of Guam's Liberation Day, commemorating the end of World War II occupation. The festival spans two days and features parades, cultural performances, food stalls, and fireworks. Dive into the historical and cultural significance of Liberation Day as Guam honors its resilience and freedom.

FestPac (June 22-July 4)

Plan your visit around the Pacific Festival of Arts, known as FestPac, a grand gathering of Pacific nations celebrating cultural exchange. Taking place from June 22 to July 4, FestPac showcases traditional arts, dance, music, and crafts from across the Pacific. Immerse yourself in the rich diversity of Pacific cultures during this dynamic event.

Guam Micronesia Island Fair (April 28-30)

April brings the Guam Micronesia Island Fair, a three-day celebration highlighting the cultural diversity of the Micronesian region. Taking place from April 28 to 30, the fair features traditional dance performances, local crafts, culinary delights, and interactive exhibits. It's an excellent opportunity to experience the broader Micronesian heritage.

Guam BBQ Block Party (TBD - Typically August)

Indulge in a culinary feast at the Guam BBQ Block Party, a lively event showcasing Guam's love for barbecued delights. Though the specific date may vary (typically held in August), this street party atmosphere brings together local BBQ enthusiasts, live music, and a variety of grilled specialties. Join the festivities for a flavorful night out.

Guam International Film Festival (September 27-October 1)

Film enthusiasts, mark your calendars for the Guam International Film Festival, taking place from September 27 to October 1. This cinematic event showcases international and local films, offering a platform for emerging filmmakers. Immerse yourself in the world of storytelling through film against the backdrop of Guam's unique setting.

Guam Ko'ko' Road Race (TBD - Typically November)

Lace up your running shoes for the Guam Ko'ko' Road Race, an annual event that promotes conservation efforts for the endangered Guam kingfisher bird, known locally as Ko'ko'. While the specific date is usually announced later in the year (typically held in November), participating in this race allows you to contribute to environmental awareness while enjoying the scenic routes of Guam.

Guam Christmas Lights Festival (December 1-January 7)

Wrap up your year with the enchanting Guam Christmas Lights Festival, transforming the island into a festive wonderland from December 1 to January 7. Experience the magic of illuminated displays, live performances, and holiday-themed events. The festival adds a touch of holiday cheer to Guam's warm tropical atmosphere.

As you plan your visit, consider aligning your travel dates with these festivals and events to enhance your cultural immersion and create lasting memories of Guam's dynamic and festive spirit.

Traditional Arts and Crafts

Guam's rich cultural heritage is beautifully expressed through its traditional arts and crafts. Immerse yourself in the island's creative spirit as you explore local markets, workshops, and artisanal spaces, discovering the craftsmanship that has been passed down through generations.

Beadwork and Shell Jewelry at Gef Pago Chamorro Village

Venture to Gef Pago Chamorro Village, where local artisans showcase intricate beadwork and shell jewelry. Admire the craftsmanship of necklaces, earrings, and bracelets, often featuring designs inspired by Chamorro motifs. Purchase a unique piece to carry a part of Guam's artistic heritage with you.

Black Coral Jewelry at Tumon Sands Plaza

Tumon Sands Plaza is a haven for those seeking exquisite black coral jewelry. Local artisans skillfully craft unique pieces using Guam's precious black coral. Explore the shops to find beautifully designed rings, pendants, and earrings, each telling a story of the island's marine treasures.

Latte Stone Carvings at Jeff's Pirates Cove

Jeff's Pirates Cove is not only known for its culinary delights but also for its showcase of Latte Stone carvings. Local artists carve these iconic Chamorro symbols from limestone, creating intricate sculptures that pay homage to Guam's ancient past. Explore the collection and perhaps acquire a piece that resonates with you.

Traditional Weaving at Valley of the Latte

Journey to the Valley of the Latte, where traditional Chamorro weaving takes center stage. Skilled artisans demonstrate the art of weaving using local materials, creating vibrant baskets, mats, and other woven items. Engage with the weavers to gain insights into the cultural significance of their craft.

Pottery at Creative Indeed Art Studio

Unleash your creativity at the Creative Indeed Art Studio, where local artists offer pottery workshops. Experience the therapeutic art of pottery-making and craft your unique piece under the guidance of skilled instructors. It's an opportunity to not only witness but actively participate in Guam's artistic traditions.

Coconut Leaf Weaving at Chamorro Cultural Village

Delve into the art of coconut leaf weaving at the Chamorro Cultural Village. Local craftsmen showcase the traditional technique of creating baskets, hats, and decorative items from coconut fronds. Witness the intricate process and, if inclined, try your hand at this ancient Chamorro skill.

Local Art Galleries in Hagåtña

Hagåtña, Guam's capital, is home to various art galleries where local artists display their works. Explore these galleries to find paintings, sculptures, and mixed-media pieces that reflect Guam's contemporary art scene. Engage with artists to gain a deeper understanding of their inspirations.

Woodcarvings at Skinner Plaza

Skinner Plaza, in the heart of Hagåtña, hosts artisans specializing in woodcarvings. Discover the intricate details of Chamorro-style woodcarvings depicting traditional motifs and cultural symbols. These handcrafted pieces serve as both artistic expressions and meaningful souvenirs.

Lågu or Storytelling Mats at Talofofo Bay

Talofofo Bay offers a unique experience with local artisans crafting Lågu, storytelling mats. These mats are woven with intricate designs that often tell stories of Chamorro culture and traditions. Engage with the weavers to gain insights into the symbolism woven into each piece.

Lime and Coconut Shell Art at Agana Shopping Center

Agana Shopping Center is a hub for lime and coconut shell art. Local artists transform lime and coconut shells into stunning pieces of art, often featuring traditional Chamorro patterns. Explore the shops to find distinctive wall hangings and sculptures that showcase Guam's cultural aesthetics.

As you explore Guam's traditional arts and crafts scene, let each creation be a window into the island's cultural legacy.

Chapter 7

Practical Travel Information

Transportation Options

Embarking on a journey to Guam in 2024 means diving into an island paradise with a myriad of transportation options to enhance your exploration. Understanding the diverse ways to navigate the island ensures a seamless and enjoyable travel experience.

Airport Arrival

Upon landing at Antonio B. Won Pat International Airport (GUM), Guam's main gateway, you'll find yourself at the heart of the island's transportation network. The airport, equipped with modern facilities, serves as the starting point for your Guam adventure.

Rental Cars

To truly explore Guam at your own pace, renting a car is a convenient and popular option. Major rental car companies have a presence at the airport, offering a range of vehicles to suit your preferences. With well-maintained roads and clear signage, navigating the island becomes a breeze.

Public Transportation

Guam's public transportation system provides a cost-effective way to traverse the island. Buses, known as "lechon," operate on designated routes, covering key areas. While public buses are a budget-friendly option, they may have limited schedules, so plan your itinerary accordingly.

Taxis and Rideshare

Taxis are readily available in Guam, providing door-to-door service. Additionally, rideshare services have gained popularity, offering a convenient alternative. Both options are ideal for those who prefer not to drive or want a more personalized travel experience.

Shuttle Services

Various shuttle services cater to specific routes and destinations, providing shared transportation for travelers. These can be a practical choice for airport transfers or reaching popular tourist spots. Check schedules and availability to align with your itinerary.

Walking and Biking

In certain areas, especially in tourist-centric locations and scenic spots, walking or biking becomes a delightful means of transportation. Guam's pedestrian-friendly paths and dedicated biking trails offer an eco-friendly way to explore the surroundings at a leisurely pace.

Water Transportation

Given Guam's coastal beauty, water transportation adds an exciting dimension to your travel options. Ferry services connect

Guam to neighboring islands, providing opportunities for island-hopping adventures. Additionally, boat tours offer a unique perspective of Guam's coastline.

Air Travel Within Micronesia

For those with a spirit of adventure, consider exploring other Micronesian islands. Domestic flights connect Guam to nearby destinations, offering a chance to extend your journey and discover more of the Pacific's diverse landscapes.

Accessibility Considerations

Guam is committed to ensuring accessibility for all travelers. The airport and major tourist facilities adhere to accessibility standards, and transportation providers offer services to accommodate various needs. Informing service providers in advance ensures a smoother experience for travelers with specific requirements.

Guided Tours and Excursions

To enhance your travel experience, consider joining guided tours and excursions. These not only provide transportation but also offer valuable insights from knowledgeable guides. Whether exploring historical sites or embarking on outdoor adventures, guided tours add an informative layer to your journey.

Navigation Apps and Maps

Maximize your autonomy by utilizing navigation apps and maps designed for Guam. These tools assist in real-time navigation, ensuring you don't miss out on hidden gems or take scenic detours based on your preferences.

Local Etiquette and Customs

Understanding local transportation etiquette enhances your travel experience. When using public transportation, it's customary to greet the driver upon boarding and thank them upon disembarking. Taxis and rideshare drivers appreciate clear communication regarding your destination and preferred route.

Sustainable Transportation Practices

Embrace sustainable travel by considering eco-friendly transportation options. Walking, biking, and supporting environmentally conscious transportation services contribute to the preservation of Guam's natural beauty for future generations.

Navigating Guam's transportation landscape in 2024 opens up a world of possibilities for exploration. By incorporating these transportation options into your itinerary, you can tailor your journey to match your preferences and embark on a memorable adventure through the captivating landscapes of Guam.

Day Trip to Neighboring Islands

Embarking on a day trip to the neighboring islands promises an enriching extension to your Guam adventure. Below is a detailed guide on how to get there, suggested itineraries, and approximate costs in US dollars.

Rota

How to Get There

Air Travel: Book a short flight from Guam International Airport to Rota International Airport. Flights typically take around 45 minutes, providing a convenient and quick way to reach this charming island.

Itinerary

Morning (8:00 AM - 12:00 PM): Upon arrival, explore Rota's historical sites, including the Rota Latte Stone Quarry and As Nieves Latte Site. Delve into the island's indigenous history while enjoying the serene surroundings.

Lunch (12:00 PM - 1:30 PM): Relish local cuisine at one of Rota's eateries. Try the Chamorro empanadas or seafood specialties for an authentic taste of the island.

Afternoon (1:30 PM - 4:30 PM): Head to the scenic Teteto Beach for relaxation and snorkeling. The crystal-clear waters and vibrant marine life make it an ideal spot for aquatic enthusiasts.

Evening (4:30 PM - 6:00 PM): Visit the popular Songsong Village and stroll through its picturesque streets. Experience the laid-back atmosphere and interact with locals.

Approximate Cost (per person):

- Round-trip Flight: $150 - $200
- Lunch: $20 - $30
- Snorkeling Gear Rental: $10 - $20
- Miscellaneous Expenses: $20

Saipan

How to Get There

Air Travel: Opt for a direct flight from Guam International Airport to Saipan International Airport. Flights take approximately 1.5 hours, making it a feasible option for a day trip.

Itinerary

Morning (8:00 AM - 12:00 PM): Begin your day at the historic Garapan Street Market, where local vendors offer fresh produce and handmade crafts. Immerse yourself in the vibrant market atmosphere.

Lunch (12:00 PM - 1:30 PM): Explore Saipan's diverse culinary scene by trying local delicacies at a restaurant in Garapan. Sample indigenous dishes for a flavorful experience.

Afternoon (1:30 PM - 4:30 PM): Visit the Last Command Post Park, a World War II historical site, to learn about Saipan's role in the Pacific theater. Enjoy the panoramic views of the island from this vantage point.

Evening (4:30 PM - 7:00 PM): Conclude your day with a relaxing visit to Micro Beach. Unwind on the sandy shores or take a dip in the Pacific Ocean before heading back to Guam.

Approximate Cost (per person):

- Round-trip Flight: $200 - $250
- Lunch: $25 - $40
- Entrance Fees (if applicable): $10 - $20
- Miscellaneous Expenses: $20

Tinian

How to Get There

Air Travel: Book a short flight from Guam International Airport to Tinian International Airport. Flights usually take around 30 minutes, providing a quick and convenient journey to Tinian.

Itinerary

Morning (8:00 AM - 12:00 PM): Begin your day at the House of Taga, an ancient Chamorro site with standing stones. Explore the archaeological wonders and absorb the historical significance.

Lunch (12:00 PM - 1:30 PM): Enjoy a meal at one of Tinian's local eateries, savoring Chamorro and international cuisine. Tinian is known for its delectable food scene.

Afternoon (1:30 PM - 4:30 PM): Visit the North Field, a World War II historical site. Explore the remnants of the airfield and gain insights into Tinian's role in history.

Evening (4:30 PM - 6:00 PM): Conclude your visit with a stroll along the serene beaches of Tinian. Relax as you take in the coastal beauty before heading back to Guam.

Approximate Cost (per person)

- Round-trip Flight: $120 - $150
- Lunch: $15 - $25
- Entrance Fees (if applicable): $5 - $10
- Miscellaneous Expenses: $15

Pagan

How to Get There

Charter Flights: Due to Pagan's remote location, consider chartering a flight from Guam International Airport to Pagan. Charter services are available, providing a unique and scenic journey.

Itinerary

Morning (8:00 AM - 12:00 PM): Explore Pagan's volcanic landscapes, starting with a visit to Mount Pagan. Hike to vantage points for breathtaking views of the island and surrounding ocean.

Lunch (12:00 PM - 1:30 PM): Pack a picnic lunch to enjoy amidst Pagan's natural wonders. Ensure you have sufficient provisions, as dining options are limited on the island.

Afternoon (1:30 PM - 4:30 PM): Discover the flora and fauna unique to Pagan by exploring its trails. The island's isolation has led to the evolution of distinct ecosystems.

Evening (4:30 PM - 7:00 PM): Conclude your Pagan adventure by watching the sunset from a scenic viewpoint. Capture the beauty of the twilight hours before your return journey.

Approximate Cost (per person)

- Charter Flight: $500 - $800 (approximate, as costs may vary)
- Picnic Supplies: $20 - $30
- Miscellaneous Expenses: $10 - $15

Important Tips

- Charter Flights: Ensure to book charter flights well in advance, considering the limited availability.
- Weather Considerations: Be mindful of weather conditions, especially for remote islands like Pagan, and plan accordingly.
- Permits and Permissions: Check and obtain any necessary permits or permissions for visiting specific sites on these Islands.
- Local Currency: While USD is widely accepted, it's advisable to carry some local currency for small purchases.

Embarking on a day trip to these islands expands your horizon, offering a blend of history, natural beauty, and unique landscapes. Customize your itinerary to align with your interests and embrace the opportunity to explore these lesser-known Pacific paradises.

Accommodation Options

Hotels and Resorts

Guam offers a diverse range of hotels and resorts, each catering to different preferences and budgets. Below are specific options, their locations, and approximate costs in US dollars per night.

The Westin Resort Guam

- Location: Tumon Bay, a prime beachfront location.
- Cost: $200 - $300 per night (varies based on room type and season).
- Highlights: Luxurious amenities, multiple dining options, and direct access to the beach.

Outrigger Guam Beach Resort

- Location: Tumon Bay, offering panoramic ocean views.
- Cost: $180 - $250 per night (depending on room category and availability).
- Highlights: Spacious accommodations, family-friendly facilities, and proximity to shopping and entertainment.

Hyatt Regency Guam

- Location: Tumon Bay, adjacent to shopping and entertainment areas.
- Cost: $220 - $320 per night (may vary with room selection and booking dates).

- Highlights: Modern design, on-site dining options, and a stunning pool overlooking the bay.

Dusit Thani Guam Resort

- Location: Northern part of Tumon Bay, with scenic ocean views.
- Cost: $250 - $350 per night (subject to room availability and seasonal rates).
- Highlights: Thai-inspired luxury, multiple dining venues, and a spa for relaxation.

Hilton Guam Resort & Spa

- Location: Located on Tumon Bay's beachfront.
- Cost: $180 - $280 per night (prices may vary based on room type and time of booking).
- Highlights: Extensive amenities, diverse dining choices, and a private beach area.

Nikko Guam Hotel

- Location: Tumon Bay, near Pleasure Island entertainment complex.
- Cost: $160 - $240 per night (depending on room selection and booking timing).
- Highlights: Japanese-themed accommodations, oceanfront views, and a range of dining options.

Guam Reef Hotel

- Location: Tumon Bay, within walking distance to shopping and dining.
- Cost: $150 - $220 per night (prices fluctuate based on room type and seasonal demand).

- Highlights: Modern rooms, a variety of restaurants, and access to Tumon's vibrant nightlife.

Booking Tips

- Advance Reservations: Secure your stay by booking in advance, especially during peak tourist seasons.
- Package Deals: Some hotels offer packages that include meals or additional amenities; explore these for potential savings.
- Membership Discounts: Check for membership discounts (AAA, military, etc.) that may apply to your chosen hotel.

Guesthouses and Bed & Breakfasts (B&Bs)

For a more intimate and locally immersive experience, guesthouses and Bed & Breakfasts (B&Bs) in Guam offer unique stays with a personal touch. Explore the following options, their locations, and approximate costs in US dollars per night.

Tropical Serenade

- Location: Harmon, providing a residential feel away from the bustling tourist areas.
- Cost: $80 - $120 per night (prices vary based on room type and occupancy).
- Highlights: Cozy atmosphere, personalized service, and a garden setting.

Ladysmith Bed & Breakfast

- Location: Mangilao, offering a blend of tranquility and proximity to local attractions.
- Cost: $90 - $130 per night (subject to room selection and booking dates).

- Highlights: Homely ambiance, hearty breakfast options, and easy access to hiking trails.

Asu Smokehouse & Guesthouse

- Location: Merizo, a coastal village providing a serene escape.
- Cost: $70 - $100 per night (prices fluctuate based on room availability and seasonal demand).
- Highlights: Ocean views, a communal atmosphere, and proximity to Cocos Island.

Oceanview Hotel & Residences

- Location: Yona, overlooking the Pacific Ocean.
- Cost: $85 - $120 per night (depending on room type and booking period).
- Highlights: Comfortable accommodations, personalized service, and a scenic environment.

Villa Romero

- Location: Agat, a residential area with a local vibe.
- Cost: $75 - $110 per night (prices may vary based on room occupancy and time of booking).
- Highlights: Charming setting, communal spaces, and easy access to Agat Marina.

Booking Tips

- Direct Communication: Consider reaching out directly to the guesthouses for potential discounts or special arrangements.
- Local Recommendations: Ask hosts for local insights and recommendations; they often provide valuable tips on hidden gems and authentic experiences.

- Flexible Dates: If your travel dates are flexible, inquire about off-peak rates for potential savings.

Guesthouses and B&Bs in Guam offer a more personalized and immersive experience, allowing you to connect with the island on a deeper level. From coastal retreats to residential havens, these accommodations provide a unique perspective for travelers seeking a homely environment during their stay.

Budget-Friendly Accommodations

For travelers seeking wallet-friendly options without compromising on comfort, Guam offers budget-friendly accommodations. Explore the following choices, their locations, and approximate costs in US dollars per night.

Santa Fe Hotel

- Location: Tamuning, a central area with easy access to shopping and dining.
- Cost: $60 - $90 per night (prices vary based on room type and availability).
- Highlights: Affordable rates, basic amenities, and proximity to Guam's main attractions.

Pacific Bay Hotel

- Location: Tamuning, offering a convenient location near Tumon Bay.
- Cost: $50 - $80 per night (depending on room category and booking dates).
- Highlights: Budget-friendly rates, comfortable accommodations, and accessibility to Tumon's attractions.

Harmon Loop Hotel

- Location: Harmon, a residential area with a local ambiance.
- Cost: $55 - $75 per night (subject to room availability and seasonal fluctuations).
- Highlights: Economical rates, a relaxed atmosphere, and proximity to local markets.

Hotel Santa Fe

- Location: Tamuning, close to shopping centers and entertainment.
- Cost: $65 - $95 per night (prices may vary based on room selection and booking timing).
- Highlights: Budget-friendly accommodations, friendly service, and a central location.

Mai'Ana Airport Plaza

- Location: Tamuning, particularly suitable for those needing proximity to the airport.
- Cost: $50 - $70 per night (depending on room type and booking period).
- Highlights: Affordable rates, practical amenities, and convenience for early or late flights.

Booking Tips

- Flexible Dates: Consider adjusting your travel dates for potentially lower rates during off-peak periods.
- Package Deals: Some budget-friendly accommodations offer package deals that include meals or additional amenities.
- Group Discounts: If traveling with a group, inquire about group rates for additional savings.

These budget-friendly accommodations in Guam provide practical and economical choices for travelers who prioritize affordability without compromising on a comfortable stay. With various options across different areas, you can find the perfect balance between cost and convenience during your visit.

Yoga Retreats in Guam

Guam provides an ideal backdrop for rejuvenating yoga retreats. As you explore the island's holistic offerings, immerse yourself in the world of yoga with these detailed insights into Guam's yoga retreats.

Discovering Guam's Yoga Scene

Guam's yoga scene has evolved, embracing both locals and travelers seeking a harmonious blend of relaxation and self-discovery. The island's unique energy, coupled with a burgeoning interest in wellness, has given rise to a variety of yoga retreats catering to different preferences and skill levels.

Variety of Retreat Settings

In Guam, you'll find yoga retreats set against diverse backdrops, each contributing to a distinct experience. Coastal retreats harness the soothing sounds of the ocean, providing a tranquil escape. Inland retreats, surrounded by lush greenery, offer a secluded and grounding ambiance. Whether you prefer the rhythmic waves or the serenity of nature, Guam's yoga retreats cater to your preference.

Expert-led Sessions

Guam's yoga retreats feature expert instructors who guide you through immersive sessions. These instructors often have a deep understanding of various yoga disciplines, including Hatha, Vinyasa, and Kundalini. Regardless of your experience level, you'll find sessions tailored to your needs, fostering a sense of inner peace and physical well-being.

Connecting with Nature

Yoga retreats in Guam seamlessly integrate with the island's natural beauty. Picture yourself practicing sun salutations as the sun rises over the Pacific Ocean or engaging in evening meditation surrounded by the calming sounds of tropical birds. These experiences align with Guam's commitment to providing a holistic connection between mind, body, and nature.

Wellness Beyond Asanas

Beyond traditional yoga poses, Guam's retreats often incorporate holistic wellness practices. You may find workshops on mindfulness, nutrition, and holistic healing, enriching your retreat experience. The goal is to provide a comprehensive approach to well-being that extends beyond the yoga mat and into your daily life.

Retreat Accommodations

Guam's yoga retreats offer varied accommodation options, ensuring a comfortable and nurturing environment. From beachfront resorts to eco-friendly lodges, you can choose a setting that resonates with your preferences. Imagine waking up to the gentle sea breeze or the calming rustle of leaves, enhancing your overall retreat experience.

Community and Camaraderie

Participating in a yoga retreat in Guam is not just a solitary experience; it's an opportunity to connect with like-minded individuals. Whether you're a solo traveler or joining with friends, the retreat community often fosters a sense of camaraderie. Share experiences, insights, and laughter, creating lasting connections that extend beyond the duration of the retreat.

Customized Retreat Experiences

Guam's yoga retreats recognize that each participant is on a unique journey. Therefore, many retreats offer customizable experiences. Tailor your retreat by choosing specific classes, wellness workshops, or additional activities that align with your personal goals. This personalized approach ensures that your time in Guam is not just a retreat but a transformative experience tailored to your needs.

Planning Your Yoga Retreat in Guam

If you're considering a yoga retreat in Guam, here are practical steps to guide you:

Research Retreat Options

Explore the various yoga retreats available in Guam. Consider the setting, type of yoga offered, and the overall philosophy of the retreat to find one that aligns with your preferences.

Check Instructor Credentials

Ensure that the retreat's instructors are certified and experienced. This guarantees a high-quality and safe yoga experience.

Review Accommodation Choices

Look into the accommodation options provided by the retreat. Whether you prefer a beachside villa or a mountain retreat, choose accommodation that complements your ideal environment.

Plan Your Itinerary

Many yoga retreats offer a diverse schedule of activities. Plan your daily itinerary, considering yoga sessions, wellness workshops, and any additional excursions or downtime you may desire.

Pack Mindfully

Pack comfortable yoga attire, a reusable water bottle, and any personal items needed for your retreat. Consider the climate and any specific requirements mentioned by the retreat organizers.

Embrace the Experience

Once you arrive in Guam, embrace the full experience of your yoga retreat. Immerse yourself in the sessions, connect with fellow participants, and allow the transformative energy of the island to guide your journey.

Embarking on a yoga retreat in Guam is not just a physical journey but a soulful exploration. Let the island's energy inspire your practice, and may your retreat be a harmonious blend of self-discovery, wellness, and the unparalleled beauty of Guam.

Yoga Centers in Guam

Guam boasts several yoga centers that cater to a diverse range of practitioners. Explore the following detailed insights into specific yoga centers, their locations, and associated costs in dollars.

Tranquil Waves Yoga Studio

- Location: Tumon, Guam
- Cost: Drop-in classes start at $15, Packages available
- Description: Tranquil Waves Yoga Studio, nestled in the heart of Tumon, offers a calming oasis for yoga enthusiasts. The

studio provides a variety of classes, including Vinyasa and Yin yoga. With its beachside location, you can enjoy the gentle sea breeze during your practice, creating a harmonious blend of nature and wellness.

Zen Sanctuary Yoga Studio

- Location: Tamuning, Guam
- Cost: Membership plans start at $80 per month
- Description: Zen Sanctuary Yoga Studio, situated in Tamuning, is known for its holistic approach to yoga and wellness. The studio offers a range of classes, from beginner-friendly sessions to advanced practices. Membership plans provide flexibility, allowing you to attend multiple classes per week, making it an affordable option for those committed to regular practice.

Island Bliss Yoga Retreats

- Location: Various locations in Guam
- Cost: Retreat packages start at $300 for a weekend
- Description: Island Bliss Yoga Retreats stand out for their mobile approach, offering immersive yoga experiences at various scenic locations across Guam. From beachside retreats to mountain escapes, each location provides a unique backdrop for your practice. Retreat packages typically include accommodation, meals, and a diverse schedule of yoga sessions.

Harmony Haven Wellness Center

- Location: Dededo, Guam
- Cost: Single classes at $20, Monthly packages available

- Description: Harmony Haven Wellness Center, located in Dededo, focuses on fostering a sense of balance and well-being. The center offers a range of yoga classes, including Hatha and Kundalini yoga. Single classes are accessible for drop-ins, and affordable monthly packages cater to those seeking a more consistent practice.

Pacific Asanas Yoga Collective

- Location: Agana, Guam
- Cost: Donation-based classes, suggested donation of $10-$15
- Description: Pacific Asanas Yoga Collective operates on a unique model, offering donation-based classes to make yoga accessible to all. Located in Agana, this collective emphasizes community and inclusivity. Suggested donations ensure that classes remain affordable, making it an excellent option for those on a budget.

EcoYoga Guam

- Location: Yona, Guam
- Cost: EcoYoga Retreats start at $400 for a weekend
- Description: EcoYoga Guam provides a unique experience by combining yoga with an eco-friendly ethos. Located in Yona, their retreats include sustainable practices, organic meals, and eco-conscious accommodations. While retreats have a higher initial cost, the comprehensive packages cover not only yoga sessions but also an eco-conscious lifestyle experience.

Yoga by the Sea

- Location: Agat, Guam
- Cost: Beach Yoga Sessions at $12 per class

- Description: Yoga by the Sea offers a distinctive experience with its beachside location in Agat. The classes take place right on the sand, allowing you to connect with nature during your practice. The cost for beach yoga sessions is reasonable, making it an inviting option for those looking to combine the therapeutic benefits of yoga with the calming influence of the ocean.

Sunrise Serenity Yoga

- Location: Piti, Guam
- Cost: Sunrise Yoga Sessions at $18 per class
- Description: For those seeking an early morning practice, Sunrise Serenity Yoga in Piti offers invigorating sessions against the backdrop of Guam's sunrise. The classes emphasize mindfulness and energizing flows, providing a perfect start to your day. Drop-in rates for sunrise sessions make it convenient for both locals and visitors.

Island Flow Yoga Lounge

- Location: Mangilao, Guam
- Cost: Unlimited Monthly Pass at $120
- Description: Island Flow Yoga Lounge, situated in Mangilao, is known for its dynamic and engaging classes. The unlimited monthly pass allows enthusiasts to attend as many classes as desired, making it an attractive option for those committed to regular practice. The lounge ambiance adds a touch of relaxation to your yoga experience.

Yoga Retreats at Luxury Resorts

- Location: Various luxury resorts in Guam
- Cost: Package prices vary; starting at $500 for a weekend

- Description: Several luxury resorts in Guam offer exclusive yoga retreat packages for those seeking a blend of wellness and indulgence. These retreats often include premium accommodations, spa treatments, and gourmet meals alongside daily yoga sessions. While on the higher end of the cost spectrum, these packages provide a luxurious escape for yoga enthusiasts.

Flowing Harmony Yoga Collective

- Location: Yigo, Guam
- Cost: Class packages start at $50 for five classes
- Description: Flowing Harmony Yoga Collective in Yigo focuses on creating a harmonious community through yoga. With class packages designed to accommodate various schedules, this collective is a great option for individuals looking to incorporate yoga into their routine without a long-term commitment. The emphasis is on creating a supportive and inclusive space for all.

Gentle Yoga for Seniors

- Location: Various community centers
- Cost: Seniors' yoga classes are often free or donation-based
- Description: Guam recognizes the importance of yoga for individuals of all ages. Various community centers offer gentle yoga specifically tailored for seniors. These classes, often free or donation-based, provide a supportive environment for older individuals to enhance flexibility, balance, and overall well-being.

Corporate Yoga Programs

- Location: Various workplaces and business districts

- Cost: Corporate packages vary; contact providers for quotes
- Description: Recognizing the benefits of workplace wellness, several yoga instructors and studios in Guam offer corporate yoga programs. These programs bring yoga directly to workplaces, providing employees with stress relief and mindfulness tools. Costs depend on the size and requirements of the corporate group.

Yoga for Kids and Families

- Location: Dededo, Tamuning, and Agana
- Cost: Family packages are available; starting at $30 per family
- Description: Families in Guam can engage in yoga together with specialized classes catering to kids and parents. These sessions, offered in various locations, focus on creating a fun and bonding experience through yoga. Family packages make it an affordable and enjoyable activity for all.

Specialized Yoga Workshops

- Location: Rotating locations; check workshop schedules
- Cost: Workshop fees vary; typically starting at $25 per session
- Description: Guam's yoga community often hosts specialized workshops focusing on specific aspects of yoga, such as inversions, mindfulness, or therapeutic practices. These workshops, held in rotating locations, provide an opportunity to deepen your understanding of yoga beyond regular classes.

These yoga centers in Guam provide a spectrum of choices, ensuring that practitioners of all levels and preferences can find a suitable space to enhance their well-being.

Essential Travel Essentials

As you prepare for your Guam adventure, ensuring you have the right travel essentials enhances the overall experience. Here's a comprehensive checklist to help you stay organized and well-prepared:

Travel Documents

- Passport and copies
- Visa (if required)
- Flight itinerary
- Hotel reservations
- Travel insurance details
- Emergency contacts

Health and Safety

- Personal medications and prescriptions
- Basic first aid kit
- Insect repellent
- Sunscreen (consider high SPF)
- Reusable water bottle

Electronics

- Power adapter and converter
- Mobile phone and charger
- Camera and accessories
- Portable charger/power bank

Clothing and Accessories

- Lightweight, breathable clothing
- Comfortable walking shoes

- Swimwear
- Hat and sunglasses
- Rain jacket or poncho

Personal Items

- Toiletries (toothbrush, toothpaste, etc.)
- Travel-sized laundry detergent
- Quick-dry towel
- Personal hygiene products
- Travel-sized sewing kit

Travel Gear

- Lightweight backpack or daypack
- Money belt or neck pouch
- Luggage locks
- Travel pillow
- Portable umbrella

Financial Essentials

- Credit/debit cards
- Some cash in local currency
- Travel wallet or organizer
- Budget planner or expense tracker

Entertainment and Navigation

- Guidebook or Guam travel guide (like this one)
- Language translation app
- Entertainment (books, e-reader, or music player)
- Guam maps or navigation app

Snacks and Refreshments

- Snack bars or trail mix
- Reusable snack containers
- Collapsible water bottle
- Instant coffee or tea packets

Miscellaneous

- Lightweight travel blanket or shawl
- Ziplock bags (for organizing and waterproofing)
- Notepad and pen
- Small sewing kit
- Multi-tool or Swiss Army knife

Tips for Packing

- Check Weather Forecasts: Ensure your clothing is suitable for Guam's climate during your visit.
- Pack Versatile Items: Choose clothing and accessories that can be mixed and matched for various occasions.
- Limit Toiletries: Opt for travel-sized toiletries or consider purchasing essentials upon arrival to save luggage space.

By considering these essential travel items, you'll be well-equipped for a comfortable and enjoyable stay in Guam. Tailor this checklist to your specific needs and preferences, ensuring a hassle-free and memorable journey.

Language and Communication

Useful Phrases in Chamorro

Embarking on your journey to Guam brings an exciting opportunity to immerse yourself in the local culture, and one of the best ways to do this is by familiarizing yourself with Chamorro, the indigenous language of Guam. Here, I'll provide you with useful phrases in Chamorro, accompanied by pronunciation patterns, to enhance your communication and connect with the people of Guam on a deeper level.

Common Greetings and Politeness

- Håfa adai (HAH-fuh day): Hello/What's up?
- Buenas (BWEH-nahs): Good morning/afternoon/evening.
- Ñot hao (nyot how): How are you?
- Biba (BEE-bah): Live/long live.
- Dangkolo na si Yu'os Ma'åse' (DAN-kolo na see YOO-ohs mah-AH-say): Thank you very much.

Pro Tip: When meeting someone for the first time, a warm "Håfa adai" sets a friendly tone, while "Buenas" is a versatile greeting throughout the day.

Basic Expressions and Responses

- Un tungo' (oon TOONG-oh): I understand.
- Ti hu tungo' (tee hoo TOONG-oh): I don't understand.
- Si Yu'os mamåna (see YOO-ohs mah-MAH-nah): God bless you.
- Fan håo yan hågu (fan how yan hah-goo): Me and you.
- Manhåfåfo (man-HAH-fah-fo): Excuse me/sorry.

Pro Tip: "Un tungo'" and "Ti hu tungo'" will be your allies in various situations, ensuring effective communication.

Getting Around and Directions

- Hågu (HAH-goo): Here.
- Åya (AH-ya): There.

- Kåo (KAH-oh): Where.
- Estå (ES-tah): Is it far?
- Loffan (LOH-fahn): Near.

Pro Tip: "Estå" is handy when asking about distance, while "Hågu" and "Åya" help you orient yourself in a new location.

Eating and Dining Etiquette

- Kåo mangga? (KAH-oh mang-ga): What is this?
- Kumånat ham? (koo-MAH-naht hahm): Did you eat?
- Man matakho' (mahn mah-TAH-ko): I'm full.
- Si Yu'os mamahålang (see YOO-ohs mah-mah-HAH-lang): Bon appétit!
- Mangnga (mang-ngah): Delicious.

Pro Tip: Asking "Kåo mangga?" is a delightful way to delve into the local culinary scene, and expressing "Mangnga" signifies your appreciation for a delicious meal.

Shopping and Bargaining

- Kao ti ha' (kah-oh tee hah): Too expensive.
- Mungnga' maolek (mung-ngah mah-OH-lek): It's very nice.
- Kao ti ya-hu (kah-oh tee YAH-hoo): I don't want it.
- Båba (BAH-bah): How much?
- Mamatngon (mah-MAHT-ngohn): Beautiful.

Pro Tip: "Båba" is your go-to phrase when exploring local markets, and "Mamatngon" expresses admiration for handcrafted items.

Emergencies and Health Concerns

- Ayudå-mu (ah-YU-dah-moo): Help me.
- Man hihilo' (mahn hee-HEE-lo): I'm lost.

- Man hasso (mahn HAH-so): I'm sick.
- Lågu (LAH-goo): Water.
- Lågu kottura (LAH-goo koh-TOO-rah): Boiled water.

Pro Tip: "Man hasso" is essential if you need assistance with health matters, and "Lågu kottura" ensures you get safe drinking water.

Cultural Interaction and Respect

- Håyi (HAH-yee): Sir/Madam.
- Si Yu'os ma'åse' (see YOO-ohs mah-AH-say): Thank you.
- Kao hu tungo' (kah-oh hoo TOONG-oh): I don't understand.
- Åtten i lina'la' (AH-ten ee lee-NAH-lah): Please wait.
- Dankulo na si Yu'os (DAN-koo-loh na see YOO-ohs): God bless.

Pro Tip: "Håyi" shows respect, and "Dankulo na si Yu'os" is a gracious way to express gratitude.

Socializing and Making Friends

- Måtenña na sinånan-mu (MAH-ten-nyah na see-NAH-nahn-moo): What is your name?
- Håyi hao? (HAH-yee how): Who are you?
- Må'åse' (mah-AH-say): Welcome.
- Kao un hågu (kah-oh oon HAH-goo): I like you.
- Si Yu'os mamahålang (see YOO-ohs mah-mah-HAH-lang): Cheers!

Pro Tip: Initiating conversations with "Måtenña na sinånan-mu" is a friendly way to start, and "Må'åse'" is a warm welcome.

Numbers and Counting

- Mekkachin (MEH-kah-cheen): One.

91

- Månotlo' (MAH-not-lo): Two.
- Tulu (TOO-loo): Three.
- Fåtsan (FAHT-sahn): Four.
- Lima (LEE-mah): Five.

Pro Tip: Mastering basic numbers like "Mekkachin" to "Lima" will prove helpful in various situations, from shopping to organizing transportation.

Weather and Seasons

- Ålas (AH-lahs): Hot.
- Fria (FREE-ah): Cold.
- Manhåo guaha na chenchule' (mahn-HAH-oh gwah-HAH nah chen-CHOOL-eh): It's raining.
- Någu manmåtae gi puti puti (HAH-goo mahn-MAH-tai gee POO-tee POO-tee): It's sunny.
- Mumu' ni' unai (MOO-moo nee OO-nai): It's windy.

Pro Tip: Knowing weather phrases like "Manhåo guaha na chenchule'" helps you plan outdoor activities accordingly.

Expressions of Time

- Guma' (GOO-mah): Morning.
- Hålomtåno' (HAH-lohm-TAH-no): Afternoon.
- Gof takpå'lo' gi isla (GOF tahk-PAH-lo gee EES-lah): Until next time.
- Kao siña yahgu (KAH-oh see-nyah YAH-hoo): I will see you later.
- Kao tuge' (KAH-oh TOO-geh): I'm leaving.

Pro Tip: Understanding time expressions ensures effective communication, especially when coordinating plans with locals.

Expressions of Agreement and Disagreement

- Ñålang (NYAH-lang): Yes.
- Ti hu na' (tee hoo NAH): No.
- Åtten i halom tåsi (AH-ten ee HAH-lohm TAH-see): Hold on a moment.
- Maolek (mah-OH-lek): Good.
- Fan un hit (fan oon hit): I like it.

Pro Tip: "Ñålang" and "Ti hu na'" are essential for clear communication, and "Maolek" is a positive expression of agreement.

Expressions of Emotion

- I minagof (ee mee-NAH-gof): I'm happy.
- Grief (gree-ef): Sad.
- Gumihit (GOO-mee-hit): Angry.
- Fina'tinas (fee-nat-EE-nas): Excited.
- Mahålang (mah-HAH-lang): Love.

Pro Tip: Expressing emotions with phrases like "I minagof" and "Fina'tinas" adds a personal touch to your interactions.

Expressions of Gratitude

- Si Yu'os mamahålang (see YOO-ohs mah-mah-HAH-lang): Thank you.
- Måpas (mah-PAS): You're welcome.
- Dangkolo na si Yu'os (DAN-kolo na see YOO-ohs): God bless you.
- Mungnga' ma'åse' (mung-ngah mah-AH-say): Thank you very much.
- Manana'sin håo (mah-NAH-nas-sin hah-oh): I appreciate it.

Pro Tip: Expressing gratitude with sincerity using phrases like "Mungnga' ma'åse'" fosters positive connections.

Expressions for Celebrations

- Biba Guåhan (BEE-bah GWAH-han): Long live Guam.
- Felis Kaskålas (FEH-lis kahs-KAH-las): Merry Christmas.
- Felis Kwanza (FEH-lis KWAN-zah): Happy New Year.
- Mås yahgu giya i korona (mahs YAH-hoo gee-ya ee koh-ROH-nah): Happy Birthday.
- Pascua (PAS-kwah): Easter.

Pro Tip: Participate in local celebrations by using phrases like "Biba Guåhan" and "Felis Kaskålas" to join in the festive spirit.

Expressions for Farewell

- Ådios (AH-dyos): Goodbye.
- Hågu un linibre (HAH-goo oon lee-NEE-bray): Take care.
- Tåya' gi i båbyu-hu (TAI-ya gee ee BAH-bee-hoo): See you tomorrow.
- Månu na'fåtai (MAH-noo nah-FAH-tai): Until we meet again.
- Dångkulo na si Yu'os (DAN-koo-loh na see YOO-ohs): God bless you.

Pro Tip: Leaving with a warm farewell using phrases like "Månu na'fåtai" ensures a positive closing to your interactions.

Expressions for Common Interactions

- Ñålang (NYAH-lang): Yes.
- Ti hu na' (tee hoo NAH): No.
- Si Yu'os mamahålang (see YOO-ohs mah-mah-HAH-lang): Thank you.
- Buenas (BWEH-nahs): Good morning/afternoon/evening.

- Håfa adai (HAH-fuh day): Hello/What's up?

Pro Tip: Being familiar with these common phrases ensures smooth interactions in various situations.

Expressions for Compliments

- Mamatngon (mah-MAHT-ngohn): Beautiful.
- Guinaiya (gween-eye-ya): Gorgeous.
- Må'o (MAH-oh): Handsome.
- Manmåno' (mahn-MAH-noh): Cute.
- Maolek (mah-OH-lek): Good.

Pro Tip: Offering genuine compliments using phrases like "Guinaiya" and "Manmåno'" fosters positive connections.

Expressions for Small Talk

- Håfa tatatmanu-hu? (HAH-fah tah-TAHT-mah-noo-hoo): What is your hobby?
- Måolek i lunghi-hu (mah-OH-lek ee LOONG-ee-hoo): My day is good.
- Håyi-hu (HAH-yee-hoo): My friend.
- Munga' (MOO-ngah): See you.
- Si Yu'os ma'åse' (see YOO-ohs mah-AH-say): Thank you.

Pro Tip: Initiating small talk using phrases like "Håfa tatatmanu-hu?" allows you to connect with locals on a personal level.

Expressions for Exploring and Adventure

- Bai hu tungo' (bye hoo TOONG-oh): Let's go.
- Bai hu estudiå (bye hoo es-tu-DYAH): Let's explore.

Discussing the Environment

- Is it safe to swim here? - Maolek bai i silebra i sinåkan gi i tiempongue? (mah-oh-lek by ee see-leh-bra ee see-nah-kahn gee ee tee-em-pong-ge)
- Where can I find recycling bins? - Yu'us dónde i tiempongue ni' halom tåno'? (yoos don-dee ee tee-em-pong-ge nee hah-lom tah-noh)

Expressions of Surprise

- Oh, really? - Ai, lao! (ai, la-oo)
- That's amazing! - Magof! (mah-gof)

Discussing Food Preferences

- Do you have vegetarian options? - Ti man-måñaina i tiempongue ni' månnge'? (tee mahn-mah-nye-nah ee tee-em-pong-ge nee mang-ge)
- I'm allergic to... - Gui'åhan-hu put alergia para... (gwee-ah-han-hoo put ah-lehr-hee-ah pah-rah)

Interacting at Cultural Events

- When is the next cultural event? - Ki maolek na tiempo gi i este na lå'u? (kee mah-oh-lek nah tyem-po gee ee eh-steh nah la-oo)
- Where can I experience traditional Chamorro dance? - Yu'us dónde i tiempongue ni' fannani Chamorro? (yoos don-dee ee tee-em-pong-ge nee fan-nah-nee cha-moh-roh)

Conversing with Children

- Hi, little friend! - Håfa små'måmi? (hah-fah smah-mah-mee)
- What's your favorite game? - Ki manåo-hu gi i lepblo-mu? (kee mah-nao-hoo gee ee lep-blo-moo)

Expressions for Special Moments

- Congratulations on your wedding! - Biba i gubetmu! (bee-bah ee goo-bet-moo)
- Best wishes for the future! - Magof na espesiat finatinas-hu! (mah-gof nah es-peh-syat fee-na-tee-nas-hoo)

Socializing

- What's your phone number? - Ki na'bendisiyon-mu i numbu di telefono-hu? (kee nah-ben-dee-syon-moo ee noom-boo dee teh-leh-foh-no-hoo)
- Let's meet again - Mågo'i tano' (mah-goh-ee tah-noh)
- Can I take a photo? - Fanatgai yu' put fumoto? (fah-na-tai yoo put foo-moh-toh)
- What's your email address? - Ki na'bendisiyon-mu i mekdek? (kee nah-ben-dee-syon-moo ee mek-dek)

Understanding Chamorro Culture

- Tell me more about Chamorro culture - Maolek-maolek put fakmåmi gi i che'lu Chamorro (mah-oh-lek mah-oh-lek put fahk-mah-mee gee ee chay-loo cha-moh-roh)
- Can you teach me a Chamorro song? - Fanmatto-hu i kanta Chamorro? (fahn-ma-toh-hoo ee kahn-tah cha-moh-roh)

Celebrations and Special Occasions

- Happy Birthday! - Felis Cumpleaños! (feh-lees koom-pleh-ah-nyos)
- Merry Christmas! - Felis Navidad! (feh-lees nah-vee-dahd)
- Congratulations! - Biba! (bee-bah)

At the Beach

- Where is the nearest beach? - Yu'us dónde i tiempongue niyok? (yoos don-dee ee tee-em-pong-ge nee-yok)
- Can you recommend a good snorkeling spot? - Ki man-magof na snotkelån-hu spot? (kee mahn-ma-gof nah snot-kel-ahn-hoo spot)

Itinerary

Weekend Itinerary

Friday: Arrival and Island Welcome

Your Guam weekend adventure begins as you touch down on this Pacific paradise. After settling into your accommodation, start your exploration with a visit to Tumon Bay. This vibrant area sets the tone for your weekend, offering a mix of shopping, dining, and entertainment. Take a stroll along the picturesque Tumon Beach, where the rhythmic waves and golden sands welcome you to the island.

Evening: Sunset Dinner at Pleasure Island

As the sun begins its descent, head to Pleasure Island for a memorable dinner experience. This entertainment hub boasts an array of restaurants, ensuring you find the perfect spot to savor a delectable meal while soaking in the sunset views. From international cuisine to local flavors, Pleasure Island caters to diverse palates.

Saturday: Nature and Adventure

Morning: Explore Two Lovers Point

Start your day with a visit to Two Lovers Point, an iconic cliffside lookout offering breathtaking panoramic views of the Pacific Ocean. Immerse yourself in the legend of two lovers who leaped from the cliff, and enjoy the serene atmosphere that surrounds this cultural landmark.

Afternoon: Adrenaline Rush at Tarza Water Park

For an afternoon filled with excitement, head to Tarza Water Park. Whether you're a thrill-seeker or seeking a more relaxed experience, the park offers a variety of water activities and attractions. From exhilarating slides to lazy river floats, Tarza Water Park caters to all ages and preferences.

Evening: Sunset Cruise from Hagåtña

As the day transitions to evening, embark on a sunset cruise from Hagåtña. Cruise along the coastline, witnessing the changing hues of the sky as the sun sets over the Pacific. This leisurely experience provides a unique perspective of Guam's beauty from the water.

Sunday: Cultural Exploration

Morning: Visit the Guam Museum

Dive into Guam's rich history by spending your morning at the Guam Museum. Explore exhibits that showcase the island's cultural heritage, from ancient Chamorro artifacts to contemporary art installations. Gain insights into Guam's journey through time and the influences that have shaped its identity.

Afternoon: Chamorro Village Experience

For a true taste of Chamorro culture, head to Chamorro Village in Hagåtña. The Sunday Market is a vibrant showcase of local crafts, delicious cuisine, and live performances. Engage with local artisans, sample traditional dishes, and enjoy the lively atmosphere that defines Chamorro Village.

Evening: Farewell Dinner with a View

Conclude your weekend with a memorable farewell dinner at a seaside restaurant. Opt for one of the establishments along the coastline, where you can enjoy a delicious meal with the soothing sounds of the ocean as your backdrop. Reflect on your weekend filled with natural wonders, adventures, and cultural discoveries.

This weekend itinerary is designed to offer a well-rounded experience of Guam, combining relaxation, adventure, and cultural exploration.

Five-Day Itinerary

Day 1: Arrival and Tumon Bay Welcome

Morning: Arrival and Tumon Bay Exploration

As you land on the island, kick off your five-day adventure with a visit to Tumon Bay. Explore the charming beachfront, indulge in a leisurely breakfast at a local cafe, and take in the panoramic views that set the stage for your Guam experience.

Afternoon: Relaxation at Ypao Beach Park

For a tranquil afternoon, head to Ypao Beach Park. Unwind on the pristine sands, take a dip in the crystal-clear waters, and enjoy the serene atmosphere surrounded by lush greenery. It's the perfect spot to acclimate to the island's laid-back pace.

Evening: Sunset Dining at Beachfront Restaurants

Choose one of the beachfront restaurants along Tumon Bay for a captivating sunset dining experience. Enjoy a delightful meal with the rhythmic sounds of the waves as your soundtrack.

Day 2: Nature and Adventure

Morning: Hike to Fonte Plateau

Embark on a morning hike to the Fonte Plateau. The trail offers spectacular views of Guam's landscape, providing a peaceful retreat into nature. Capture the beauty of the island from elevated vantage points.

Afternoon: Underwater Adventure at Fish Eye Marine Park

Spend your afternoon exploring the vibrant marine life at Fish Eye Marine Park. Whether you choose to snorkel or take a ride on the underwater observatory, this marine park offers a unique perspective of Guam's underwater wonders.

Evening: BBQ Dinner at a Local Grill

Wrap up your adventurous day with a laid-back barbecue dinner at a local grill. Indulge in Guam's barbecue specialties, savoring the flavors of the island in a relaxed setting.

Day 3: Historical Insights

Morning: Visit Fort Nuestra Señora de la Soledåd

Delve into Guam's history with a visit to Fort Nuestra Señora de la Soledåd. Explore the well-preserved structures and learn about the island's colonial past. The fort offers a glimpse into Guam's strategic significance over the centuries.

Afternoon: Explore Plaza de España

Stroll through Plaza de España in Hagåtña, the capital city. Admire the historical architecture, including the Statue of Chief Kepuha, and soak in the ambiance of this central square.

Evening: Cultural Dinner and Dance Performance

Immerse yourself in Chamorro culture during an evening dinner featuring traditional cuisine and dance performances. Experience Guam's vibrant heritage in a lively and engaging setting.

Day 4: Scenic Landscapes

Morning: Jeep Tour to Southern Guam

Embark on a jeep tour to explore the scenic landscapes of southern Guam. Visit viewpoints like Cetti Bay Overlook and Jeff's Pirate's Cove, capturing the diverse beauty of the island.

Afternoon: Beach Day at Ritidian Point

Spend your afternoon at Ritidian Point, a stunning beach surrounded by natural beauty. Relax on the white sands, swim in the clear waters, and appreciate the untouched landscape.

Evening: Sunset at Asan Bay Overlook

Witness a mesmerizing sunset at Asan Bay Overlook, providing a breathtaking view of the western coast. Reflect on your Guam journey against the backdrop of vivid colors painting the sky.

Day 5: Farewell and Departure

Morning: Last-Minute Shopping in Tumon

Before bidding farewell to Guam, indulge in some last-minute shopping in Tumon. Explore the boutiques and souvenir shops, picking up mementos to remember your island getaway.

Afternoon: Guam National Wildlife Refuge Visit

Conclude your Guam adventure with a visit to the Guam National Wildlife Refuge. Connect with nature one last time, appreciating the diverse flora and fauna that call Guam home.

Evening: Farewell Dinner with Ocean Views

For your final evening, choose a seaside restaurant for a farewell dinner. Enjoy a delicious meal as you gaze upon the ocean, reminiscing about the memories created during your five days in Guam.

This five-day itinerary is crafted to provide a well-rounded experience, allowing you to explore Guam's nature, history, and culture while savoring its scenic landscapes and vibrant atmosphere.

Two-Week Itinerary

Day 1-2: Arrival and Tumon Bay Welcome

Day 1

Morning: Arrive in Guam and settle into your accommodation.

Afternoon: Explore Tumon Bay, visit local shops, and enjoy a beachfront dinner.

Evening: Relax at Tumon Beach and take in the first sunset of your stay.

Day 2

Morning: Morning swim at Ypao Beach Park, followed by breakfast with ocean views.

Afternoon: Visit UnderWater World for an interactive marine experience.

Evening: Sunset dinner cruise for a different perspective of Guam's coastline.

Day 3-4: Nature and Adventure

Day 3

Morning: Hike to Fonte Plateau for panoramic views of the island.

Afternoon: Explore Tarza Water Park for a mix of water adventures.

Evening: BBQ dinner at a local grill.

Day 4

Morning: Snorkel at Fish Eye Marine Park for a unique underwater experience.

Afternoon: Discover the lush landscapes of Nimitz Hill and visit the Micronesia Mall.

Evening: Cultural dinner at a traditional Chamorro restaurant.

Day 5-7: Historical and Cultural Exploration

Day 5

Morning: Tour Fort Nuestra Señora de la Soledåd for historical insights.

Afternoon: Explore Hagåtña's Plaza de España and surrounding historical sites.

Evening: Cultural dinner with traditional dance performances.

Day 6

Morning: Visit the Guam Museum for a comprehensive look at the island's history.

Afternoon: Chamorro Village experience for local crafts and cuisine.

Evening: Attend a local festival or event if scheduled.

Day 7

Morning: Scenic drive to southern Guam, stopping at viewpoints like Cetti Bay Overlook.

Afternoon: Relax at Ritidian Point Beach.

Evening: Sunset at Asan Bay Overlook followed by dinner.

Day 8-10: Scenic Landscapes

Day 8

Morning: Jeep tour to explore the southern landscapes and visit Jeff's Pirate's Cove.

Afternoon: Afternoon at Agana Shopping Center for a mix of shopping and local eats.

Evening: Dinner at a beachfront restaurant in Tumon.

Day 9

Morning: Island-wide exploration with stops at various parks and viewpoints.

Afternoon: Ritidian Point Nature Preserve for wildlife appreciation.

Evening: Sunset at Pagat Cave.

Day 10

Morning: Guided hike to the stunning Pagat Arch.

Afternoon: Leisure time for reflection and relaxation.

Evening: Seafood dinner at a seaside restaurant.

Day 11-14: Extended Explorations

Day 11-14

Explore the Micronesia region: Consider a day trip to nearby islands.

Water Adventures: Snorkeling, diving, or paddleboarding.

Cultural Immersion: Attend local workshops or community events.

Relaxation: Spend time on less-explored beaches for a peaceful retreat.

Day 14: Farewell and Departure

Day 14

Morning: Last-minute shopping for souvenirs in Tumon.

Afternoon: Visit the Guam National Wildlife Refuge for a nature walk.

Evening: Farewell dinner at a favorite local restaurant, reminiscing about your unforgettable Guam journey.

Thus, these itineraries are designed to offer a comprehensive and immersive exploration of Guam, allowing you to discover the island's diverse landscapes, rich history, and vibrant culture while enjoying a mix of relaxation and adventure. Adjustments can be made based on personal preferences and any special events happening during your stay.

Final Thoughts and Recommendations

As you conclude your exploration of the "Guam Travel Guide 2024: Your Essential Companion for Exploring the Natural Beauty, Outdoor Activities, History, and Culture," it becomes evident that this guide is not merely a compendium of information; it's an invitation to embark on a transformative journey through the enchanting island of Guam. Let's delve into the comprehensive insights, encapsulating the essence of Guam's allure and the guide's role as your indispensable companion.

A Range of Natural Beauty Unveiled

Guam's natural beauty, showcased in this guide, unfolds like a vibrant treasure waiting to be explored. From the pristine beaches that caress the shores with crystal-clear waters to the lush forests and scenic landscapes that paint the island's canvas, each section invites you to immerse yourself in the untouched wonders of Guam. The guide acts as your compass, directing you to the most breathtaking vistas and unveiling the secrets of the island's diverse ecosystems.

Dynamic Outdoor Adventures Await

For the adventure seeker, Guam in 2024 is a playground of possibilities. The guide illuminates the realm of outdoor activities, from heart-pounding adventure sports to serene water excursions and picturesque hiking trails. Whether you're craving an adrenaline rush or a leisurely exploration of Guam's terrain, the guide stands as your gateway to a plethora of outdoor adventures, ensuring that every moment on the island is infused with excitement and discovery.

107

A Journey Through Guam's Rich History

Guam's history, intricately woven into its landscapes, is a narrative waiting to be explored. The guide leads you through historical landmarks that bear witness to the island's colonial past, cultural heritage sites that echo the voices of generations, and indigenous traditions that form the very fabric of Chamorro identity. As you traverse through time, the guide's historical insights enrich your understanding of Guam, transforming your journey into a profound exploration of the island's heritage.

Immersing in Cultural Vibrancy

Immerse yourself in Guam's rich cultural heritage through the guide's exploration of culinary delights, festivals, and traditional arts and crafts. The culinary section invites you to savor the diverse flavors that define Guam's gastronomic scene, while the festivities and events capture the island's lively spirit. Delve into the world of traditional arts and crafts, where skilled artisans weave stories through their creations. The guide ensures that your cultural immersion is not a spectatorship but an active participation in Guam's vibrant traditions.

Practical Travel Wisdom for Seamless Exploration

While the allure of Guam's beauty and culture captivates, the guide is equally committed to ensuring your practical travel needs are met seamlessly. The section on practical travel information serves as your logistical ally, offering transportation tips, accommodation options, and essential travel essentials. Navigating Guam becomes an effortless experience, allowing you to focus on the essence of your journey rather than logistical complexities.

Yoga Retreats

Among the gems within the guide is the detailed exploration of Yoga Retreats in Guam. Guam's serene landscapes set the stage for transformative yoga experiences, and the guide directs you to specific retreats catering to diverse preferences. From beachside tranquility to mountain seclusion, each retreat becomes a holistic oasis where expert-led sessions, connection with nature, and wellness beyond asanas converge. The guide doesn't just inform; it becomes your companion in creating a rejuvenating escape that transcends the ordinary.

Guam 2024: A Unique Chapter Unfolding

In contemplating your journey through the Guam Travel Guide 2024, it's crucial to recognize that this edition is not static; it's a snapshot of a unique chapter in Guam's story. The year 2024 brings with it a blend of timeless charm and contemporary influences. The guide, crafted with precision and foresight, ensures that you navigate Guam with relevance and insight, embracing the island's evolving spirit.

Final Recommendations

As you prepare to set foot on Guam, armed with the knowledge and insights provided by this guide, a few recommendations emerge:

Embrace the Diversity

Guam's beauty lies in its diversity. Embrace the opportunity to explore the varied landscapes, engage with different cultural facets, and savor the richness of experiences that Guam offers.

Immerse Yourself

Beyond being a spectator, become an active participant in Guam's cultural scene. Whether it's joining a local festival, trying traditional dishes, or attending a yoga retreat, immerse yourself in the vibrant culture of Guam.

Connect with Nature

Guam's natural wonders are not just scenery; they are invitations to connect with nature. Whether you're strolling on pristine beaches or hiking through lush forests, take moments to pause, absorb, and appreciate the profound beauty surrounding you.

Customize Your Experience

The guide offers a wealth of information, but your journey is uniquely yours. Customize your experience by selecting activities and destinations that resonate with your interests. Let Guam unfold in a way that aligns with your travel aspirations.

Embrace Wellness

If the Yoga Retreats section resonates with your interests, consider incorporating wellness practices into your Guam journey. Whether it's a yoga session on the beach or a retreat in the mountains, Guam's natural serenity provides an ideal backdrop for rejuvenation.

Stay Informed

While the guide is comprehensive, staying informed about any updates or additional offerings is advisable. Local events, new attractions, or evolving travel conditions can enhance your experience, and staying informed ensures you don't miss out on any opportunities.

In conclusion, the Guam Travel Guide 2024 serves as more than a compendium of information; it's a portal to a transformative experience. Guam, with its natural beauty, rich history, and dynamic cultural vibrancy, awaits your exploration. Let this guide be your constant companion, guiding you through every facet of Guam's allure and ensuring that your journey is nothing short of extraordinary. As you embark on this adventure, may Guam captivate your senses, enrich your soul, and leave an indelible mark on your travel narrative. Safe travels, and may Guam unfold its wonders before you in 2024.

Acknowledgments

My special thanks go to the people of the Guam for their warm hospitality, openness, and willingness to share their beautiful home with travelers from around the world. Your kindness has made this guide more than just a collection of information; it's a reflection of the heart and soul of Guam.

I want to acknowledge you, the traveler. Your curiosity, enthusiasm, and willingness to explore this incredible destination have made this journey worthwhile. I hope this guide has enriched your Guam experience and provided you with the tools to create lasting memories in this remarkable part of the world.

As you venture forth on future adventures, may you carry the spirit of Guam with you, and may your travels be filled with the same wonder, appreciation, and discovery that you've found here.

Guam Travel Planner 2024

Guam

Travel Planner 2024

Date:_____

Town:_____

Monday	Tuesday	Wednesday

Thursday	Friday	Saturday

Checklist	Note

Guam Travel Guide 2024

Guam

Travel Planner 2024

Date:_____

Town:_____

Monday	Tuesday	Wednesday

Thursday	Friday	Saturday

Checklist	Note

Guam

Travel Planner 2024

Date:_____

Town:_____

Monday	Tuesday	Wednesday

Thursday	Friday	Saturday

Checklist	Note

Travel Planner 2024

Monday	Tuesday	Wednesday

Thursday	Friday	Saturday

Checklist	Note

Guam

Travel Planner 2024

Date:_____

Town:_____

Monday	Tuesday	Wednesday

Thursday	Friday	Saturday

Checklist	Note

| Date:_____ |
| Town:_____ |

Travel Planner 2024

Monday	Tuesday	Wednesday

Thursday	Friday	Saturday

Checklist	Note

Guam Travel Itinerary 2024

Name:

Duration of Stay:

Hotel Name:

Flight No:

Arrival Date:

Days	What To Do	Budget
01		
02		
03		
04		
Note		

Name:		Duration of Stay:
Hotel Name:		
Arrival Date:		Flight No:

Days	What To Do	Budget
01		
02		
03		
04		
Note		

Name:		Duration of Stay:

Hotel Name:

Flight No:

Arrival Date:

Days	What To Do	Budget
01		
02		
03		
04		
Note		

Name:		Duration of Stay:
Hotel Name:		Flight No:
Arrival Date:		

Days	What To Do	Budget
01		
02		
03		
04		
Note		

Name:		Duration of Stay:
Hotel Name:		
Arrival Date:		Flight No:

Days	What To Do	Budget
01		
02		
03		
04		
Note		

Name:		Duration of Stay:
Hotel Name:		
Arrival Date:		Flight No:

Days	What To Do	Budget
01		
02		
03		
04		
Note		

Made in United States
Troutdale, OR
09/17/2024

22906546R00076